ROASTING *The Swan of Avon*

Shakespeare's
Redoubtable
Enemies
& Dubious
Friends

Bruce R. Smith

Published by the
Folger Shakespeare Library, Washington, D.C.
in conjunction with an exhibition entitled
"Roasting the Swan of Avon"
March 1– June 4, 1994

This volume has been published in conjunction with the exhibition *Roasting the Swan of Avon: Shakespeare's Redoubtable Enemies and Dubious Friends*, on display at the Folger Shakespeare Library, Washington, D.C., from March 1 to June 4, 1994.

Major funding for the exhibition and publication comes from the Lila Wallace-Reader's Digest Fund.
This publication is also supported by the Andrew W. Mellon Publication Fund.

Edited by Rachel Doggett, Andrew W. Mellon Curator of Books

Publication Director: Janet Alexander Griffin, Director of Museum and Public Programs
Production Coordinator: Jane E. Bissonnette
Designed by Jeanne Krohn
Photography by Julie Ainsworth
Typesetting by Barbara Shaw

Printed in the United States
ISBN 0-295-97364-1

Cover: detail from Joseph Clayton Clarke, "G.B. Shaw 'Cutting' Shakespeare in Hades," watercolor and ink on paper

Acknowledgments

Something of the congeniality, wit,

and learning of the many people who contributed to this project comes across,

I hope, in the pages that follow. Putting the whole thing together was a group venture, and all the more fun for that. The idea to show off some of the Folger's satiric prints came originally from Werner Gundersheimer, Director of the Folger Shakespeare Library. Credit for the title goes to Georgianna Ziegler, Reference Librarian, who offered many inspired suggestions for what should be included, chased down dozens of details, and arranged for the borrowing of several items. The array of unusual art objects on view here—among them a rolling pin, a drinking mug, and a porcelain statue of Shakespeare wearing britches seldom seen since the demise of Rococo—comes courtesy of Jean Miller, Art Reference Librarian. Rosalind Larry, Assistant Reading Room Supervisor, provided prompt and patient research assistance at every stage. The uniform clarity of the photographs of so many diverse items, of so many sizes, in so many different media, is due to the technical skill of Julie Ainsworth, Head of Photography. Preparation of items for exhibit, and the mounting of the show itself, was expertly handled by Frank Mowery, Head of the Conservation Department, and members of the conservation staff. For factual advice and stylistic suggestions on the text of this catalog I am grateful to Georgianna Ziegler; Randy Bass and John Pfordresher of Georgetown University; Barbara Mowat, Director of Academic Programs at the Folger Library; and Rachel Doggett, Curator of Books. Rachel Doggett's support has been crucial at every turn.

Special thanks are due to the lenders to the exhibition:
Roger Pringle, Director, and the Trustees of the Shakespeare Birthplace Trust, the National Gallery of Art in Washington, Garry Trudeau of "Doonesbury," Ward Elliott and Robert Valenza of Claremont McKenna College, John Hirsh and Zelda Teplitz of Georgetown University, and Prof.-Dr. Kuno Schuhmann of the Technische Universität, Berlin.

B.R.S.

A Roster of Roasters

Being a cultural hero isn't easy.

From his own day down to ours, William Shakespeare has had his fair share of mockers, debunkers, and deconstructors, not to mention fans who don't equate admiration with reverence. In the pages that follow, all of these people get their say. Beginning with rival playwright Robert Greene, who is reported to have called the fledgling Shakespeare "an upstart crow," and ending with postmodern critics, who have announced "the death of the author," *Roasting the Swan of Avon* exposes the backside of Bardolatry: the back-handed compliments that turned Shakespeare into an artless "natural" poet in the 17th century, the festivals, folios and forgeries that enriched 18th-century self-promoters like John Boydell, the Thomas Bowdler-izing that fathered *The Family Shakespeare* in the 19th century, the cultural pillaging of American industrialists in the 20th century, the sour grapes of rival geniuses like Voltaire, Tolstoi, and Shaw, the extraordinary lengths to which people have gone to prove that everybody but themselves has been the dupe of a massive hoax and that Shakespeare's plays were not written by Shakespeare at all.

During his own lifetime the man from Stratford (baptized 1564, buried 1616) inspired envy among his professional rivals, contempt among academics, and animosity among Puritans, but it is remarkable how many people have lent a hand at turning the spit in the centuries since his death. "Shakespeare" has figured as a powerful metaphor in a series of conflicts that the historical William Shakespeare could hardly have foreseen. Alan Sinfield catches the situation exactly:

> Shakespeare is a powerful cultural token, such that what you want to say has more authority if it seems to come through him. That is how Shakespeare comes to speak to people at different times: the plays have been continuously reinterpreted in attempts to coopt the bard for this or that worldview. This is not surprising or illegitimate; it is a key practice through which cultural contest proceeds.[1]

If cultural pundits of the 17th century felt compelled to describe Shakespeare's works as brilliant but unpolished diamonds-in-the-

1. Alan Sinfield, *Faultlines: Cultural Materialism and the Politics of Dissident Reading* (Berkeley: University of California Press, 1992), p. 11.

rough, it was because the critical principles of their own time and place made them divide up the aesthetic universe into the "artful" and the "natural." If 18th-century editors, theatrical impresarios, and print publishers invited ridicule by the earnestness with which they set about turning Shakespeare into an icon of Britishness, it was because they needed a national culture to match Britain's new middle-class prosperity—and something to rival France's claims to cultural hegemony. (If Voltaire attacked Shakespeare, it was because he knew exactly what the British were up to.) If 19th-century readers preferred to enjoy Shakespeare's plays and poems purged of all sexual improprieties—or, better still, in the form of children's stories—it was because they themselves were anxious about those very improprieties. If Thomas Nast could appropriate characters from Shakespeare for political cartoons and yet crown his career by painting *The Immortal Light of Genius*, it is because Americans have always been prone both to idolize Shakespeare and to make sport with him. Witness this book.

Eating Crow

Apart from the terse notations

of various officious clerks in various official documents, the first surviving reference to William Shakespeare is a slam. One of a series of pamphlets that cashed in on the notoriously profligate life of playwright Robert Greene when he died in 1592, *Greenes Groats-Worth of Witte, Bought with a Million of Repentance* (London: for William Wright, 1592) may in fact have been written by Henry Chettle, but it puts into Robert Greene's mouth this warning to university-educated gentlemen "that spend their wits in making plaies" and sell them to the empty-headed "Puppets" who act them:

> Yes trust them not: for there is an upstart Crow, beautified with our feathers, that with his *Tygers hart wrapt in a Players hyde*, supposes he is as well able to bombast out a blanke verse as the best of you: and beeing an absolute *Johannes fac totum*, is in his owne conceit the onely Shake-scene in a countrey. O that I might intreat your rare wits to be imploied in more profitable courses: & let those Apes imitate your past excellence, and never more acquaint them with your admired inventions. (sig. F1ᵛ)

If "Shake-scene" and "*Johannes factotum*" weren't enough to make the allusion clear, Greene (or Chettle writing in Greene's voice) parodies one of Richard's speeches in *The True Tragedie of Richarde Duke of Yorke* (London: W. W. for T. Millington, 1600), the play most commonly known today as *Henry VI, Part 3* (1.4.138–141 in modern editions):

> Oh Tygers hart, wrapt in a womans hide!
> How couldst thou draine the life bloud of the childe,
> To bid the father wipe his eyes withall,
> And yet be seene to beare a womans face? (sigs. B4–B4ᵛ)

In 1592 Shakespeare's lines would have been ringing in Londoners' ears. Usually dated among the first four or five scripts that Shakespeare wrote for the stage, *The True Tragedy of Richard Duke of York* probably joined the repertory of Strange's Men or Pembroke's Men a year before *Greene's Groatsworth of Wit* appeared.

Laurens Van Haecht Goidtsenhoven (text) and Jacob de Zetter (illustrations), *Microcosmos* (Frankfurt: Lucas Jennis, 1618), no. 68. Greene's "upstart crow" was hatched by Horace.

Why a crow? Aesop, Martial, and Macrobius all cast crows as mimics, but Greene is likely thinking quite specifically of Horace's epistle to Julius Florus (1.3), where an author who steals other authors' lines is imaged as a bird who steals other birds' feathers:

> What is Celsus at work on? Although he's been told,
> He needs to be told again to find his own stuff
> And keep his hands off the books in the Palatine Library,
> Which Apollo hospitably harbors; the rest of the flock
> Will fly up some day to strip from our bird the fine feathers
> He stole to dress up in, and make him their laughing stock.[2]

A graduate of Cambridge, Greene proudly distinguishes himself from the shabbily educated likes of William Shakespeare, "Anticks garnisht in *our* colours" (sig. F1, emphasis added). Greene may have had a point. Commercial rivalry among acting companies often meant that one company's hit became another company's knock-off. The maid-in-male-disguise, a stage trick that became one of Shakespeare's favorites, figures as a major device in Greene's romance play *James IV* (1590).

2. Horace, *Satires and Epistles*, trans. Smith Palmer Bovie (Chicago: University of Chicago Press, 1959), pp. 174-175.

A prettie newe Ballad, intytuled:

The Crowe sits vpon the wall, Please one and please all.

To the tune of, Please one and please all.

Please one and please all,
Be they great be they small,
Be they little be they lowe,
So pypeth the Crowe,
    sitting vpon a wall:
    please one and please all,
    please one and please all.

Be they white be they black,
Haue they a smock on their back,
Or a kircher on her head,
Whether they spin silke or thred,
whatsoeuer they them call :
please one and please all,
please one and please all.

Be they sluttish be they gay,
Loue they worke or loue they play,
Whatsoeuer be their chéere,
Drinke they Ale or drinke they béere,
whether it be strong or small :
please one and please all,
please one and please all.

Be they sower be they swéete,
Be they shrewish be they méeke,
Weare they silke or cloth so good,
Veluet Bonnet or French-hood,
Vppon her head a Cap or call :
please one and please all,
please one and please all.

Be they halt be they lame,
Be she Lady be she dame,
If that she doo weare a pinne,
Kéepe she tauerne or kéepe the Inne,
    Either bulke bouth or stall,
    please one and please all,
    please one and please all.

The goodwife I doo meane,
Be shée fat or be she leane,
Whatsoeuer that she be,
This the Crowe tolde me,
    sitting vppon a wall :
    please one and please all,
    please one and please all.

If the goodwife speake aloft,
Sée that you then speake soft,
Whether it be good or ill,
Let her doo what she will,
    and to kéepe your selfe from thrall,
    please one and please all,
    please one and please all.

If the goodwife be displeased,
All the whole house is diseased,
And therefore by my will,
To please her learne the skill,
    Least that she should alwaies brall:
    please one and please all,
    please one and please all.

If that you bid her doo ought,
If that she doo it not,
And though that you be her goodman,
You your selfe must doo it than,
    be it in kitchin or in hall :
    please one and please all,
    please one and please all.

Let her haue her owne will,
Thus the Crowe pypeth still,
Whatsoeuer she command,
Sée that you doo it out of hand,
    whensoeuer she doth call :
    please one and please all,
    please one and please all.

Be they wanton be they wilde,
Be they gentle be they milde:
Be shée white be she browne,
Doth she skould or doth she frowne,
    Let her doo what she shall :
    please one and please all,
    please one and please all.

Be she coy be she proud,
Speake she soft or speake she loud,
Be she simple be she flaunt,
Doth she trip or doth she taunt,
    the Crowe sits vpon the wall :
    please one and please all,
    please one and please all.

Is she huswife is she none,
Doth she drudge doth she grone,
Is she nimble is she quicke,
Is she short is she thicke,
    Let her be what she shall :
    please one and please all,
    please one and please all.

Be they ritch be they pore,
Is she honest is she whore,
Weare she cloth or Veluet braue,
Doth she beg or doth she craue,
    Weare she hat or silken call :
    please one and please all,
    please one and please all.

Be she cruell be she curst,
Come she last come she first,
Be she young be they olde,
Do they smile doo they skould,
    though they doo nought at all :
    please one and please all,
    please one and please all.

Though it be some Crowes guise,
Oftentimes to tell lyes,
Yet this Crowes words doth try,
That her tale is no lye,
    For thus it is and euer shall:
    please one and please all,
    please one and please all.

Please one and please all,
Be they great be they small,
Be they little be they lowe,
So pypeth the Crowe,
    sitting vpon a wall :
    please one and please all,
    please one and please all.

FINIS.   R.T.

Imprinted at London for Henry Kyrkham, dwelling at the little North doore of Paules, at the signe of the blacke Boy.

Richard Tarlton (attributed), "A Prettie Newe Ballad, Intytuled: The Crowe Sits upon the Wall,/ Please One and Please All" (London: for Henry Kyrkham, 1592), reproduced from the Huth Collection by permission of the British Library. Pleasing women and writing plays: the burden is the same.

In *Microcosmos*, an emblem book first published in 1579 for a pan-European market, Horace's thieving *cornicula* ("little crow") has become a *corvus* (usually a raven, but sometimes a synonym for *cornix*, or crow). The sentiments remain the same. "Presumptuous and Ambitious People" are addressed in the guise of a thieving bird:

> Tell me, crow, why you pride yourself on others' plumage.
>> Say why others' qualities please you so much.
> Before you know it, the flock of birds
>> is going to ask for it all back, and you'll be naked.
> Nobody wants to claim stolen boons as his own,
>> or wishes he had filched somebody else's honors.
> If you're smart (and I say it advisedly), you'll make sure
>> what you want is your own lot and not somebody else's.

The crow may be a mimic in Aesop and a plagiarist in Horace, but in "A Prettie Newe Ballad, Intytuled: The Crowe Sits upon the Wall,/ Please One and Please All," published the same year as Greene's pamphlet, the crow adds a way with women to his theatrical skills. Attributed to the famous clown Richard Tarlton (d. 1588), the ballad can be sung to the tune of "Please One and Please All"—which supplies the refrain, or burden, to each stanza in the new set of words:

> Be they wanton, be they wilde,
> Be they gentle, be they milde:
> Be shee white, be she browne,
> Dooth she skould or dooth she frowne,
> Let her doo what she shall:
> Please one and please all,
> Please one and please all.

Whether or not he actually wrote *Greene's Groatsworth of Wit*, Henry Chettle found himself a few months later eating crow. Several "play-makers," it seems, took offense at the remarks Greene had made from the grave. Lacking a living target, they singled out Chettle for revenge. In a preface "To the Gentlemen Readers" of *Kind-Harts Dreame* (London: for William Wright, 1593?), Chettle claims only to have copied Greene's deathbed manuscript of *Groatsworth*, not to have written the book himself. Furthermore, he is heartily sorry that he didn't strike out Greene's lines about at least one of the playwrights, "because my selfe have seene his demeanor no lesse civill than he exelent in the qualitie he professes: Besides, divers of worship have reported, his uprightnes of dealing, which argues his honesty, and his facetious grace in writting, that approves his Art" (sig. A4). Two essential features of Bardolatry first appear in this apology: Shakespeare handled his fellows honestly and his pen nimbly.

"Sweet Swan of Avon"— with a Grain of Salt

De mortuis nil nisi bonum: about the dead, speak nothing but good. In the First Folio of Shakespeare's playscripts, *Mr. William Shakespeares Comedies, Histories, & Tragedies* (London: Isaac Jaggard and Edward Blount, 1623), published seven years after the author's death, all the rivalry and rancor surrounding the upstart crow seem to have been forgotten entirely. After commendations from Shakespeare's fellow actors, John Heminges and Henry Condell, come verses "To the memory of my beloved, The Author, Mr. William Shakespeare: And what he hath left us" from fellow playwright Ben Jonson. Any suspicion that Jonson might feel anything so inappropriate as *envy* is carefully dispelled in the first line: "To draw no envy (*Shakespeare*) on thy name,/ Am I thus ample to thy Booke, and Fame" (fol. A4). Upstart crow is metamorphosed into another bird entirely:

> Sweet Swan of *Avon*! what a sight it were
> > To see thee in our waters yet appeare,
> And make those flights upon the bankes of *Thames*,
> > That so did take *Eliza*, and our *James*! (fol. A4ᵛ)

In other contexts Jonson had talked—and continued to talk— a rather different line. Salt, not sugar, was Jonson's preferred condiment. As he says of himself in the Prologue to *Volpone* (acted 1606),

> All gall, and coppresse, from his inke, he drayneth,
> > Onely, a little salt remayneth;
> Wherewith, he'll rub your cheeks, til (red with laughter)
> > They shall looke fresh, a weeke after.

Hence in the Induction to *Bartholomew Fair* (acted 1614) Jonson can be mildly contemptuous of playgoers who "will sweare, *Jeronimo*, or *Andronicus* are the best playes, yet" and proudly casts himself as a writer "loth to make Nature afraid in his *Playes*, like those that beget *Tales*, *Tempests*, and such like *Drolleries*"

Unknown artist of the mid-18th century, Portrait of Ben Jonson, possibly after Peter Oliver (1589?–1647), oil on canvas. "He is a great lover and praiser of himself, a contemner and scorner of others" is how William Drummond described Jonson after several days of conversation together in 1618. Swans, it should be noted, were famous for finding a singing voice only at the moment of death.

(*The Workes of Benjamin Jonson* [London: R. Meighen, 1640], sig. A5ᵛ–A6). So much for *Titus Andronicus*, *The Winter's Tale*, and *The Tempest*. Whether or not he knew that William Drummond was taking notes, Jonson regaled the Scottish poet with opinions on virtually every contemporary poet and playwright anyone would have heard about. According to Drummond's transcript of their conversations, held during December or January of 1618/19, Jonson found *The Winter's Tale* absurd: "Sheakspear, in a play, brought in a number of men saying they had suffered Shipwrack

Unknown late 19th-century artist, Shakespeare's coat-of-arms, oil on canvas. Heraldically at least, William Shakespeare was neither crow nor swan. In 1596 the long-standing application of Shakespeare's father for a coat-of-arms was finally granted, possibly because his playwright son paid the substantial fees involved. The bird that shakes the spear in the approved design is, in the words of the herald, "a falcon his winges displayed Argent standing on a wrethe of his coullors [*i.e.* colors]." Possessed of this new coat-of-arms, John Shakespeare and his son William could each style himself "Gentleman." Six months later William bought New Place, one of the two largest dwelling houses in Stratford-upon-Avon. To judge from the legal traces left by Shakespeare the man of property, the Falcon of New Place generally took precedence over the Swan of Avon.

in Bohemia, wher ther is no sea neer by some 100 miles." Jonson's conclusive opinion on the sweet swan of Avon? "Shakspear wanted [*i.e.* lacked] Arte." In the commonplace book that he kept, published after his death as *Timber, or Discoveries,* in *The Workes* (1641), Jonson talks about Shakespeare's artistic shortcomings at even greater length:

> *I remember*, the Players have often mentioned it as an honour to *Shakespeare,* that in his writing, (whatsoever he penn'd) hee never blotted out line. My answer hath beene, would he had blotted a thousand. Which they thought a malevolent speech. (p. 97)

Imagine that.

Railers and Scourgers

If the scurrilous poems themselves were not enough, the title page to John Davies' collected epigrams, *The Scourge of Folly*, provides graphic evidence that early modern satirists were not just being figurative when they called their poems "scourges." (See title page on p. 12.) "Folly," with his breeches down, is hoisted up on the back of "Time" (note the hourglass, the scythe, and the forelock handy for seizing before Time passes you by), in a posture perfect for being whipped by "Witt," who is exclaiming, "nay up with him if he were my brother." And a "brother" the butt of the satirist often turned out to be. Especially when the subject was drama, 17th-century satirists could be every bit as outrageous as the plays—and the playwrights—they were excoriating. Davies' epigram "*To our English Terence Mr. Will: Shake-speare*" implies that Shakespeare had come in for some *ad hominem* abuse from fellow poets. Davies' own style is gentler:

> Some say (good *Will*) which I, in sport do sing[,]
> Hads't thou not plaid some Kingly parts in sport,
> Thou hads't bin a companion for a *King*;
> And, beene a King among the meaner sort.
> Some others raile; but, raile as they thinke fit,
> Thou hast no rayling, but, a raigning Wit:
> *And* honestly *thou sow'st, which they do reape;*
> *So, to increase their Stocke which they do keepe.*
> (pp. 76–77)

John Davies makes a witty play on Shakespeare's ability to make himself a king; other writers were less amused by such transformations. Actors offered a ready object for satiric attack in part because they could amass wealth so easily and turn themselves into gentlemen overnight. In *Ratseis Ghost, or, The Second Part of His Madde Prankes and Robberies* (London: V. S[immes], sold by J. Hodgets, 1605), the robber hero delights in telling about the time he tricked some traveling London players to give back, with interest, the substantial amount of money he had given them the night before for entertaining him in an inn. To the humiliated chief player Ratsey gives this arch advice:

> thou hast a good presence upon a stage, me thinks thou
> darkenst thy merite by playing in the country: Get thee to
> London, for if one man were dead, they will have much neede

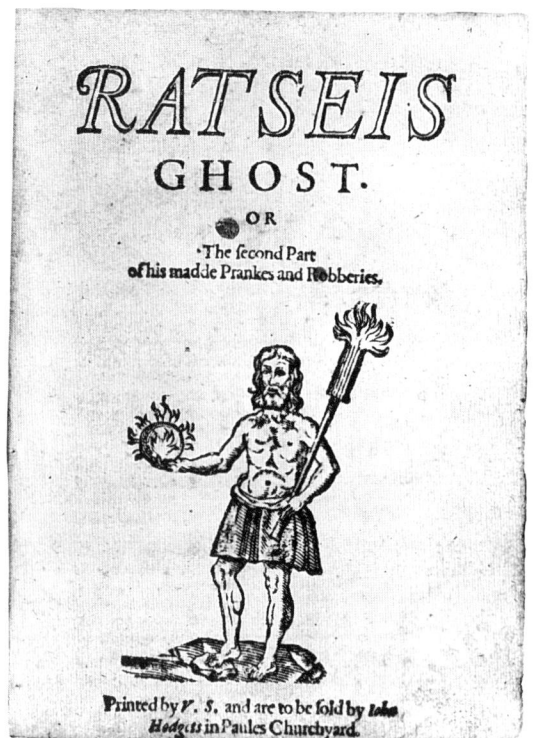

of such a one as thou art. There would be none in my opinion, fitter then thy selfe to play his parts: my conceit is such of thee, that I durst venture all the mony in my purse on thy head, to play Hamlet with him for a wager. (sig. B1)

If the *Hamlet* in question is Shakespeare's four- or five-year-old play, the actor would be Richard Burbage (1567?–1619). If the *Hamlet* in question is the lost "Ur-*Hamlet*" on which Shakespeare based his play, the actor Ratsey has in mind might be Edward Alleyn (1566–1626), who retired from the stage just about the time this pamphlet appeared (1605), bought the manor of Dulwich, and founded Dulwich College. Shakespeare himself took the rest of Ratsey's advice to heart:

> when thou feelest thy purse well lined, buy thee some place or Lordship in the Country, that growing weary of playing, thy mony may there bring thee to dignitie and reputation . . . .
> (sigs. B1–B1ᵛ)

That, of course, is just what the author of *Hamlet* did.

John Webster (1580?–1625?) made capital more quietly. "Detraction," he says, "is the sworne friend to ignorance: For mine owne part I have ever truly cherisht my good opinion of other mens worthy Labours...." In his Preface to *The White Devil* (London: N. O. for Thomas Archer, 1612), Webster goes on to list the playwrights he admires and what he admires about them:

George Chapman's style, Ben Jonson's labor, Francis Beaumont and John Fletcher's "no lesse worthy composures." Last in Webster's list comes "the right happy and copious industry of M. *Shake-speare*, M. *Decker*, & M. *Heywood*" (sig. A2ᵛ). To someone of Webster's generation (he was fourteen years younger than Shakespeare), this happy and copious threesome may have seemed outdated by 1612— but not so outdated that upstart Webster couldn't pluck quite a few feathers from Shakespeare for his own plumage. *The White Devil*, by one calculation, contains no fewer than thirty direct verbal borrowings from Shakespeare's plays.[3]

Contemporaries who railed against Shakespeare were not limited to playwrights and folk heroes. They included academics—the very sort of people who centuries later could thank Shakespeare for their livelihood. Today the Bodleian Library at Oxford contains a prized collection of 16th- and 17th-century play texts, but with no thanks to Sir Thomas Bodley, the library's founder. In a letter to the head librarian, he demanded that "baggage books"—to wit, plays, pamphlets, and almanacs—be removed from the cases. If reference to Shakespeare is here oblique, it seems much more direct in Robert Anton's *The Philosopher's Satyrs* (London: T. C. and B. A. for Roger Jackson, 1616), published in the very year of Shakespeare's death. Settled comfortably in his study in Magdalen College, Anton takes aim at *The Comedy of Errors* from an academic long range. His squib traces no shorter course than the seven celestial spheres, each of which inspires a separate satire in "a maske of sevenfold uniformity" (sig. A2ᵛ), before reaching its target under the sign of Venus:

> What *Comedies* of *errors* swell the *stage*
> With your most *publike vices*, when the *age*
> Dares personate in *action*, for, your *eies*
> Ranke *Sceanes* of your *lust*-sweating *qualities*. (p. 51)

The Comedy of Errors, let it be noted, is one of Shakespeare's most academic plays. It not only borrows a plot out of Plautus's *Menaechmi* but had its first recorded performance in an academic setting, as part of the Gray's Inn Christmas revels of 1594.

Twenty-five years after Shakespeare's death, it must have begun to seem obvious who was going to have the last word in these bouts of spleen. The anonymous author of this poem in *Wits Recreations* (London: for Humphrey Blunden, 1640) puts satiric attacks on Shakespeare firmly in the past tense:

> *Shake-speare* we must be silent in thy praise,
> 'Cause our encomion's will but blast thy Bayes,
> Which envy could not, that thou didst do well;
> Let thine own histories prove thy Chronicle. (sig. B5)

3. R. W. Dent, *Webster's Borrowing* (Berkeley: University of California Press, 1960), pp. 69–173.

Playing the Sodomite—or Worse

What Pieter Brueghel calls a "Kermesse" ("church-mass") Shakespeare and his contemporaries knew as a "church ale."

In *Histrio-Mastix. The Players Scourge, or, Actors Tragedie* (London: E. A. and W. I. for Michael Sparke, 1633), a salvo delivered ten years before Puritan opinion actually succeeded in knocking down London's public theaters, William Prynne provides a convenient list of abominations, among which plays rank near the top:

> effeminate mixed dancing
>
> dicing
>
> stage plays
>
> lascivious pictures
>
> wanton fashions
>
> face-painting
>
> health-drinking
>
> long hair; love locks; periwigs; women's curling, powdering, and cutting of their hair
>
> bonfires, New Year's gifts, May games, amorous pastorals, lascivious effeminate music, excessive laughter, luxurious disorderly Christmas-keeping, mummeries.

In addition to these abominations, Prynne objects to the way the follies of junk culture have been turned into expensive commodities:

> Some Play-books since I first undertooke this subject, are growne from *Quarto* into *Folio*; which yet beare so good a price and sale, that I cannot but with griefe relate it, they are now new-printed in farre better paper than most Octavo or Quarto *Bibles*, which hardly finde such vent as they.

A marginal note estimates the number of playscripts printed in the past two years alone at 40,000. Another note singles out the Folio of Shakespeare's plays (probably the Second) as occasion for special outrage: "Shackspeers Plaies are printed in the best Crowne paper, far better than most Bibles" (sig. **6ᵛ). In a nice

Print after Pieter Breughel the Elder, *The Village Fair of Hoboken* (1559), National Gallery of Art, Rosenwald Collection. How many of Prynne's abominations can you find in Breughel's picture?

instance of poetic justice, the Folger copy of *Histrio-Mastix* cited here eventually came into the hands of the actor John Philip Kemble (1757–1823).

Puritan tracts leave no doubt about it: theater is dangerous because it is sexually exciting. Like the satirists, Philip Stubbs in *The Anatomie of Abuses* (London: Richard Jones, 1583) loves to anatomize the very bodies he excoriates:

> . . . marke the flockyng and runnyng to Theaters and Curtens, daylie and hourelie, night and daie, tyme and tide, to see Playes and Enterludes, where suche wanton gestures, such bawdie speeches: suche laughyng and flearyng: suche kissyng and bussyng: suche clippyng and culling: such wincking and glauncing of wanton eyes, and the like is used, as is wonderfull to beholde. Then these goodly Pageantes beyng doen, every mate sortes to his mate, every one brynges an other homewarde of their waie very freendly, and in their secrete conclaves (covertly) thei plaie the *Sodomits*, or worse. And these be the fruites of Plaies and Enterludes, for the most part.

(pp. 90ᵛ–91)

Wenceslaus Hollar (1607–1677), Portrait of William Prynne (1600–1669), engraving (undated). Obsessed with the body and with the purse, Prynne believed that stage plays hit people in two spots at once.

Accomack County, Virginia, Order Book for 1663–1666, fol. 102, reproduced from the original in the Virginia State Library, Richmond. The first reference to drama in English-speaking North America, like the first reference to Shakespeare, points up the dubious place of playacting in early modern culture.

What the "worse" may be is left to the reader's imagination. Though "sodomy" in early modern English could cover deviant behavior of all sorts, Stubbs's remark has prompted more than one 20th-century commentator to think twice about the all-male composition of Shakespeare's acting company.

Objections to stage plays came over to New England with the Puritans, but as it happens the earliest surviving reference to drama in English-speaking North America occurs in Virginia. Court documents of Accomack County on Virginia's Eastern Shore for November 1665 record the arrest of three men accused by His Majesty's Attorney of "acting a play by them called the Bare and the Cubb on the 27th of August last past." Deferring the matter, the judge orders the three men to "appear the next Court

Abraham de Bruyn (1540–1587), *Omnium Pene Europae, Asiae, Aphricae... Gentium Habitus* (Antwerp: Michiel Colÿn, 1581). Puritans get their comeuppance in a number of Elizabethan and Jacobean plays, but never more hilariously than in the gulling of Malvolio in *Twelfth Night* (first recorded performance in 1601). Tricked into thinking Lady Olivia is in love with him, Malvolio appears before her with his legs flamboyantly cross-gartered, only to discover that she hates cross-gartering. This plate from Abraham de Bruyn's catalog of European fashions tells would-be style-chasers (and latter-day costume designers) how to cross-garter correctly.

Aulicus Germanus.   *Honoratioris loci famulus Germanus.*

4. Sewall's diary and letter-book, with disapproving references to drama in Boston in 1685 and 1687, are transcribed in Massachusetts Historical Society *Proceedings*, ser. 5, vol. 5 (1877): 103–104, and ser. 6, vol. 2 (1886): 29–30.

in those habilements that they then acted in, and give a draught of such verses or other Speeches and passages, which were then acted by them" (fol. 102). They did, and they were acquitted. If the offense in this case sounds suspiciously like a political lampoon (no script of "The Bear and the Cub" has survived), it was the moral offensiveness of playacting in general that caused Samuel Sewall to make note of certain incidents in Boston twenty years later.[4]

Nature Dressed . . .

For Shakespeare's reputation as a "natural" genius the credit, or the blame, ultimately belongs to Ben Jonson. In his commendatory verses to Shakespeare's First Folio (see **"Sweet Swan of Avon"—with a Grain of Salt**) Jonson praises his sometime rival for having brought Aeschylus, Sophocles, and Euripides back to life—an amazing feat, since "thou hadst small *Latine*, and lesse *Greeke*" (sig. A4). The "facetious grace in writting" that impressed Henry Chettle (see **Eating Crow**) becomes, in Jonson's self-referential scheme, the antithesis to his own learning and discipline:

> Nature her selfe was proud of his designes,
> And joy'd to weare the dressing of his lines!
> Which were so richly spun, and woven so fit,
> As since, she will vouchsafe no other Wit.
>
> (sig. A4ᵛ)

By the 18th century, Jonson's back-handed compliment had become a critical cliché, as witness George Romney's painting *The Infant Shakespeare, Attended by Nature and the Passions*, the original of which (measuring four feet eight inches by six feet nine inches) now presides over the New Reading Room of the Folger.

In the portrait that introduces John Milton's collected *Poems* (1645), "Nature" has been pushed into the perspective distance, beyond a curtain that sequesters the youthful poet inside, within a universe defined by the muses of tragedy, love poetry, astronomy, and history, whose names appear around the oval frame. Shakespeare, on the other hand, belongs in the realm beyond the curtain—or so Milton positions him in *L'Allegro* (written in 1631, eight years after Jonson had installed Shakespeare as a poet of nature). Amid a catalog of pleasures Milton asks Euphrosyne, goddess of mirth, to waft him to the theater—but only if Jonson's works or Shakespeare's are showing:

> Then to the well-trod stage anon,
> If *Jonsons* learned Sock be on,
> Or sweetest *Shakespear* fancies childe,
> Warble his native Wood-notes wilde,
> And ever against eating Cares,
> Lap me in soft *Lydian* Aires . . . .   (p. 36)

George Romney (1734–1802), *The Infant Shakespeare, Attended by Nature and the Passions*, engraved by Benjamin Smith (d. 1833), published by John and Josiah Boydell as the frontispiece to *A Collection of Prints from Pictures Painted for the Purpose of Illustrating the Dramatic Works of Shakespeare by the Artists of Great Britain* (1803). Heralded by Romney's image, everything that follows in the Boydells' engraved gallery of great moments in Shakespeare becomes testimony to the poet's "natural" genius.

William Marshall (active 1591–1649), frontispiece to John Milton, *Poems* (London: R. Raworth for H. Moseley, 1645). If Milton is in *here*, Shakespeare is out *there*.

The warbling that Milton hears may be that of a bird (if so, certainly not that of a crow or a falcon), but it also invokes the poet as a piping shepherd, an image that goes back to Virgil, Theocritus, and Hesiod. Just such a pastoral scenario is suggested in the landscape beyond the curtain.

Shakespeare had not quite departed from the world's stage before other playwrights came along who could compensate for his artistic deficiencies. John Fletcher (1579–1625), fifteen years Shakespeare's junior, collaborated with Shakespeare on *The Two Noble Kinsmen* (probably acted 1613; see **Deconstructors**), but it was with Francis Beaumont (1584–1616) that Fletcher formed the first famous team in British theatrical history. To hear John Berkenhead tell it, Beaumont and Fletcher appeared on the scene right on cue. In a commendatory poem prefaced to Beaumont and Fletcher's *Comedies and Tragedies* (London: for Humphrey Robinson and Humphrey Moseley, 1647) Berkenhead declares,

> *Shakespear* was early up, and went so drest
> As for those *dawning* houres he knew was best;
> But when the Sun shone forth, *You Two* thought fit
> To weare just Robes, and leave off Trunk-hose-Wit.
>
> (sig. E1ᵛ)

(Britches known as "trunk-hose," stuffed with wool to exaggerate the wearer's thighs, had been popular in the 16th century; to Berkenhead's cavalier taste they were decidedly old-fashioned.) Comparison must have seemed inevitable in a volume modeled so obviously on the folio of Shakespeare's collected plays, in its second edition by the time the Beaumont and Fletcher folio appeared in 1647. No less inevitable were the terms of comparison. Berkenhead's image of Shakespeare as a flowing river, naturally wandering whither it would, finds its headwaters in Ben Jonson:

> Brave *Shakespeare* flow'd, yet had his Ebbings too,
> Often above Himselfe, sometimes below;
> Thou Always Best; if ought seem'd to decline,
> 'Twas the unjudging Rout's mistake, not Thine . . . .
>
> (sig. E2)

Berkenhead's sneer about Shakespeare's "Trunk-hose-Wit" is amplified by the academic playwright William Cartwright (1611–1643) in commendatory verses on Fletcher, reprinted in Cartwright's posthumously collected works, *Comedies, Tragicomedies, with Other Poems* (London: for Humphrey Moseley, 1651) after they had also appeared in the Beaumont and Fletcher folio (1647). Compared to Fletcher's displays of wit, Shakespeare's jokes are socially maladroit—or worse:

> *Shakespeare* to thee was dull, whose best Jest lies
> I'th'Ladies questions, and the Fools replies,
> Old fashion'd wit, which walk'd from Town to Town
> In turn'd Hose, which our Fathers call'd the Clown;
> Whose wit our nice times would obsceaness call,
> And which made Bawdry pass for Comicall . . . .

Enter Ben Jonson, with a snide comparison between Shakespeare's so-called "Art" and Cartwright's "free vein":

> Nature was all his Art, thy vein was free
> As his, but without his scurility . . . . (p. 273)

Jokes that already seemed obscene in the 1640s proved to be ever more embarrassing in the course of the 18th and 19th centuries (see **Breaking the Quill**).

Samuel Ireland (d. 1800), "Stratford Church &c," mezzotint from *Picturesque Views on the Upper or Warwickshire Avon* (1795).

Stratford in Shakespeare's own day may have been an ordinary market town, but by the end of the 18th century it had become a fixture in "The Picturesque." When Samuel Ireland, print-maker and antiquarian enthusiast, came to Stratford in 1795, he found in the foreground of Shakespeare's burial place not only the requisite swans of Avon but a solitary figure who might break into woodnotes wild at any moment. Unsuccessful at uncovering any Shakespearean documents to take home as souvenirs, Ireland also found reason to welcome such documents when they later turned up in his study back in London (see **Forgery: Flattery or Fraud?**).

Just how much at home Shakespeare was in the landscape of pastoral poetry can be appreciated from one of the songs Charles Dibdin (1745–1814) wrote for the Jubilee that put Stratford-upon-Avon on the literary map and officially inaugurated Shakespeare as Britain's national poet. More august profusions graced the festival, held in Stratford in September 1769, but Dibdin's ditty "Sweet Willy O," from *Jubilee, or Shakespear's Garland* (London: John Johnston, 1769), catches the popular imagination of the time by casting Shakespeare as a lusty country lad:

> The Pride of all Nature was sweet Willy O
> the first of all Swains
> he gladden'd the Plains,
> none Ever was like the sweet Willy O.

Subsequent verses celebrate how "No Shepherd e'er pip'd like the sweet Willy O," how "All Nature obey'd him the sweet Willy O," how "when Willy dy'd, / 'Twas Nature that sighd" (p. 17).

A rather different light on Shakespeare's generative powers is provided by William D'Avenant (1606–1668). As John Aubrey (1626–1697) tells the story, D'Avenant's father ran an inn in Oxford, which just happens to be about half way between Stratford and London:

William Faithorne (1616?–1691), Portrait of William D'Avenant, after John Greenhill (1649–1676), engraving (1672). If John Aubrey is to be believed, D'Avenant claimed to be Shakespeare's "natural son."

Jo. Grenhill pinx.   W. Faithorne Sculp.

Sir William D'avenant K.

Mr. William Shakepeare was wont to goe into Warwickshire once a yeare, and did commonly in his journey lye at this house in Oxon. where he was exceedingly respected. . . . Now Sir William would sometimes, when he was pleasant over a glasse of wine with his most intimate friends—e.g. Sam. Butler (author of Hudibras) &c.—say, that it seemed to him that he writt with the very spirit that Shakespeare [wrote], and seemd contented enough to be thought his son.[5]

Even listeners not so gossipy as Aubrey took D'Avenant's claim to be more than a metaphor. That would make D'Avenant (to put it as politely as possible) Shakespeare's "natural son." The edifice in which the Act of Poetic Succession is said to have transpired still stands at Number 3 Cornmarket, though it operates today as a museum noted for its 15th- and 16th-century wall paintings.

5. John Aubrey, "Brief Lives" (MS in Ashmolean Museum, Oxford, quoted in Philip Bordinat and Sophia B. Blaydes, *Sir William Davenant* (Boston: Twayne, 1981), pp. 11–12.

. . . and Nature Redressed

[I]t must be allow'd to the present Age, that the tongue in general is so much refin'd since Shakespear's time, that many of his words, and more of his Phrases, are scarce intelligible. And of those which we understand some are ungrammatical, others course; and his whole stile is so pester'd with Figurative expressions, that it is as affected as it is obscure.

Its persnickety diction aside,

the sentiment here could have been written by a 20th-century reader weary of looking at footnotes. In fact, this complaint about Shakespeare's style appeared as early as 1679, in John Dryden's Preface to *Troilus and Cressida, or Truth Found too Late* (London: for Jacob Tonson and Abel Swall, 1679), sig. A4ᵛ. Where later scholars might be inclined to provide footnotes, Dryden as a man of the theater was inspired to more radical action: he simply did the plays over. *Troilus and Cressida*, acted by the Duke's Company at the Dorset Garden Theater in April 1679, works an alchemist's magic on Shakespeare's moldy relics, or so Richard Duke claims in his verses "To Mr. *Dryden* on his Play, Called, *Truth Found too Late*":

> *Shakespear* 'tis true this tale of *Troy* first told,
> But, as with *Ennius Virgil* did of old,
> You found it dirt but you have made it gold.
>
> (sig. A1)

That is to say, Dryden is to Shakespeare what Virgil was to Ennius, the latter-day perfecter of an archaic bard's worthy but rustic originals.

It was William D'Avenant who first taught him to admire Shakespeare, or so Dryden says in his preface to *The Tempest, or The Enchanted Island* (London: J. M. for Henry Herringman, 1670). Dryden returned the favor by collaborating in what proved to be D'Avenant's last theatrical venture. In the Prologue they provided for the play's first performances by the Duke's Company at Lisle's Tennis Court in November and December 1667, Dryden and D'Avenant put a new twist on the theme of Shakespeare-as-natural-genius by casting Shakespeare as tutor not only to witty John Fletcher but to learned Ben Jonson. If poets copy Nature, they perforce must copy Shakespeare, because Shakespeare is Nature:

Jonathan Richardson (c. 1665–1745), Portrait of John Dryden (c. 1730), pencil on vellum. The poet laureate of Restoration culture, John Dryden (1631–1700) earned his bays by vigorously cultivating poetry as political discourse, by translating all of Virgil's works into English, and by teaching characters in tragedy (Shakespeare's included) to speak in heroic couplets. In the course of his Preface to *Troilus and Cressida* the Restoration Virgil justifies his alterations to Shakespeare's plays by outlining "The Grounds of Criticism in Tragedy." "*The* grounds of criticism": one notes the definite article.

> As when a Tree's cut down the secret root
> Lives under ground, and thence new Branches shoot
> So, from old *Shakespear's* honour'd dust, this day
> Springs up and buds a new reviving Play.
> *Shakespear*, who (taught by none) did first impart
> To *Fletcher* Wit, to labouring *Johnson* Art.
> He Monarch-like gave those his subjects law,
> And is that Nature which they paint and draw.

However that may be, Dryden and Davenant are unabashed about "improving" *The Tempest* in all sorts of ways, most notably by supplying for Miranda (a woman who has never seen a man) a counterpart in Hippolito (a man who has never seen a woman). Whether, as the Prologue claims, men actors were in short supply, or whether it was impossible for Restoration audiences to imagine a man so sexually naive, the part of Hippolito was played by a woman, possibly by Jane Long, who numbered among her roles Lady Macbeth. Unlike the maids-in-male-disguise that Shakespeare always turns back into girls, Hippolito keeps his gender—and shows off her fetchingly breeched legs—to the end:

> What e're she was before the Play began,
> All you shall see of her is perfect man,
> Or if your fancy will be farther led,
> To find her Woman, it must be abed.

(sig. A4)

Among 17th- and 18th-century attempts to orchestrate Shakespeare's woodnotes wild into an artful fugue, the most famous, surely, is Nahum Tate's *The History of King Lear* (London: E. Flesher, 1681). Lear lives on. Cordelia not only lives on; she marries Edgar. That happy outcome to *King Lear* held the British stage from 1681, when Tate "reviv'd" the play "with Alterations," until 1838, when the actor William Macready (1793–1873) finally

Mr. William Shakespeares Comedies, Histories, & Tragedies. The Second Impression (London: Thomas Cotes, 1632), fragment. On this recently noticed leaf from the Second Folio of Shakespeare's plays, three literary generations have, as it were, joined hands: Shakespeare himself, Shakespeare's self-proclaimed "natural son" William D'Avenant, and one of D'Avenant's own sons, Augustine. John Dryden has signed on for good measure. The question is: why? During the month he is supposed to have signed his name, May 1651, D'Avenant was a prisoner in the Tower of London, awaiting almost certain death as a traitor to the Commonwealth. Augustine D'Avenant, who is otherwise known to history only through his appearance on a genealogical tree of the D'Avenant family in a College of Arms manuscript, could have been as young as ten years old on 22 June 1675, the date he is supposed to have signed his name. Does this leaf from a Second Folio fragment belong under **Forgery: Flattery or Fraud**?

restored to the stage something like the original texts. Best known today for writing the words to "While Shepherds Watched Their Flocks by Night," Nahum Tate (1652–1715) professes in the epistle dedicatory to *King Lear* to have found Shakespeare's play "a Heap of Jewels, unstrung and unpolisht; yet so dazling in their Disorder, that I soon perceiv'd I had seiz'd a Treasure" (sig. A2ᵛ). In the Prologue, the heap of jewels becomes a "Heap of Flow'rs"; the necklace, a garland such as "each Rustick knows . . . to Compose" (sig. A4). Whether audiences think of the play as a necklace or as a garland, Edgar's closing speech indicates just what a bijou trinket Tate has made of Shakespeare's tragedy:

> Our drooping Country now erects her Head,
> Peace spreads her balmy Wings, and Plenty Blooms.
> Divine *Cordelia*, all the Gods can witness
> How much thy Love to Empire I prefer!
> Thy bright Example shall convince the World
> (Whatever Storms of Fortune are decreed)
> That Truth and Vertue shall at last succeed. (p. 67)

Francis Hayman, design for engraving of *King Lear*, Act 3, scene 6, ink on paper, tipped in after the frontispiece to *The Works of Mr. William Shakespear*, ed. Sir Thomas Hanmer (Oxford: Oxford University Press, 1744). The Folger Library's extra-illustrated copy of the first edition of Shakespeare to be published by a university press juxtaposes the engraved illustrations with original designs by Francis Hayman (1708–1776). Even in the darkest moments on the heath, *Lear* in 18th-century guise never compromises its clarity and composure.

If, as William Cartwright claimed, Shakespeare *is* Nature (see **Nature Dressed...**), he had new issues to adjudicate in the 18th century. When George Granville adapted *The Merchant of Venice* for a production in 1701, he supplied a prologue in which the ghost of Shakespeare and the ghost of John Dryden talk about sexual morality. First Dryden berates modern audiences who prefer "*French* Grimace, Buffoons, and Mimics" to British drama:

> 'Thro Perspectives revers'd they Nature view,
> Which gives the Passions Images, not true.
> *Strephon* for *Strephon* sighs; and *Sapho* dies,
> Shot to the Soul by brighter *Sapho*'s Eyes . . . .

The ghost of Shakespeare is horrified:

> These Crimes unknown, in our less polish'd Age,
> Now seem above Correction of the Stage . . . .
>
> > (*The Jew of Venice* [London: for Bernard Lintot and B. Motte, 1732], sig. H1ᵛ)

The political message comes through loud and clear: Shakespeare is a *British* hero, and as a British hero he most certainly cannot be a sodomite. Leave such things to the French. Did Granville feel uneasy about the friendship of Bassanio and Antonio? *The Jew of Venice*, no less than *Truth Found Too Late* or *The Enchanted Island* or *The History of King Lear*, demonstrates how "improvement" can function as a form of censorship.

Breaking the Quill

The dirtiest lines in Shakespeare are probably Mercutio's taunt about Juliet: "O, Romeo, that she were, O that she were/ An open-arse, and thou a pop'rin pear" (2.1.37–38). (That's "pop'rin," as in "pop her in.") At least, that's what the actor playing Mercutio may have said from the stage. When the play appeared in print in 1597, within a year or two of its first performances, the text divulged not "an open-arse" but "an open *Et Caetera.*" When the play appeared in a longer version in the 1599 quarto, the garbled line read "open, or"—a bit of phonetic nonsense that has helped 20th-century scholars reconstruct the censored original. However, the fourth quarto of 1622, *The Most Excellent and Lamentable Tragedie, of Romeo and Juliet* (London: for John Smethwicke) repeated the original "open *Et Caetera.*" Censorship of Shakespeare's plays began, then, while Shakespeare was still writing plays. Eighteenth-century editors like Alexander Pope (1688–1744) and George Steevens (1736–1800) anticipated the editors of American high school textbooks by quietly dropping the line in question.

Anxiety about Shakespeare's indecorous moments began within a few years of his death (see **Nature Dressed...**), but it was in the late 18th century, when the discreet tyranny of the bourgeoisie gained its power, that criticism turned into crisis. New editorial principles demanded a return to the earliest texts. In the case of the sonnets, that meant abandoning John Benson's artfully expurgated version of 1640, complete with *he*'s changed to *she*'s. Suddenly there was some explaining to be done. Concerning Sonnet 20 ("A woman's face with nature's own hand painted/ Hast thou, the master-mistress of my passion"), George Steevens felt compelled to append this note in his edition of 1766: "It is impossible to read this fulsome panegryick, addressed to a male object, without an equal mixture of disgust and indignation." Edmund Malone (1741–1812), the first great Shakespeare scholar, saved the day by explaining that "such addresses to men, however indelicate, were customary in our author's time, and neither imported criminality nor were esteemed indecorous." The Folger's copy of the *Supplement to the Edition of Shakespeare's Plays Published in 1778*, ed. Edmond Malone (London: C. Bathurst,

William Shakespeare,
*The Most Excellent and
Lamentable Tragedie, of
Romeo and Juliet*
(London: for John
Smethwicke, [1622])
sig. C4ᵛ. Whatever she
or he may have made of
this "*Et Caetera*," a
17th-century owner of
the Folger's copy of
Romeo and Juliet has
taken pen in hand and
changed the title to
"Juliet and Romeo."

The most Lamentable Tragedie

 Mer. If loue be blind, loue cannot hit the marke,
Now will he fit vnder a Medler tree,
And wifh his miftreffe were that kind of fruit,
As maides call Medless when they laugh alone,
O *Romeo* that fhee were, O that fhee were
Anopen & catera, and thou a Poperin Peare.
Romeo good-night Ile to my Truccle-bed,
This Field-bed is to cold for me to fleepe,
Come fhall we goe?

 Ben. Goe then, for tis in vaine to feeke him here
That meanes not to be found.   *Exeunt.*

 Ro. He ieafts at fcarres that neuer felt a wound,
But foft, what light through yonder window breakes?
It is the Eaft, and *Iuliet* is the Sunne.
Arife faire Sunne and kill the enuious Moone,
Who is already ficke and pale with griefe,
That thou her maide at farre more faire then fhee:
Be not her maide fince fhee is enuious,
Her veftall liuerie is but ficke and greene,
And none but fooles doe weare it, caft it off:
It is my Lady, O it is my loue, O that fhee knew fhee were,
Shee fpeakes yet fhee fayes nothing, what of that?
Her eye difcourfes, I will anfwero it:
I am to bold tis not to me fhee fpeakes:
Two of the faireft ftarres in all the heauen,
Hauing fome bufines, doe entreat her eyes,
To twinckle in their fpheres till they returne,
What if her eyes were there, they in her head,
The brightneffe of her cheeke would fhame thofe ftarres,
As day light doth a lampe, her eye in heauen,
Would through the ayrie region ftreame fo bright,
That birds would fing, and thinke it were not night:
See how fhee leanes her cheeke vpon her hand,
O that I were a gloue vpon that hand,
That I might touch that cheeke.

 Iuli. Ay me

 Rom. Shee fpeakes.

            Oh

1780), in which this exchange is recorded (p. 596), was once owned by Steevens and contains manuscript annotations in his hand.

Malone's remark on Sonnet 20 may have become academic dogma, but it failed to settle the issue once and for all, as witness W. H. Auden's introduction to the New American Library edition of the sonnets (1964). Making a play on bed-secrets and Red-secrets, Auden told friends in the early 1960s that "it won't do just yet to admit that the top Bard was in the homintern"—and stood by that conviction when he wrote his preface later the same year. Shakespeare, after all, was a married man and a father.

> That we are confronted in the sonnets by a mystery rather than by an aberration is evidenced for me by the fact that men and women whose sexual tastes are perfectly normal, but who enjoy and understand poetry, have always been able to read them as expressions of what they understand by the word *love*, without finding the masculine pronoun an obstacle.
> (Shakespeare, *Sonnets*, intro.
> W. H. Auden [New York: New
> American Library, 1964], p. xxix)

If not whereof, Auden certainly knew wherefore he spoke.

An epigraph from Joseph Addison articulates both the ideal (British values) and the method (censorship) that lies behind *The Family Shakespeare* (See title page on p. 30):

> The Stage might be made a perpetual Source of the most noble and useful Entertainment, were it under proper Regulations.

Although most dictionaries credit Thomas Bowdler (1754–1825) with having given the world *The Family Shakespeare*—and hence the verb "to bowdlerize"—the four-volume first edition (1807) was in fact a project of his sister, Henrietta Maria Bowdler (1753–1830). Thomas's contribution was to expand the twenty plays covered by the first edition into the entire canon with the ten-volume edition of 1818—and to take credit for the whole affair. Like Granville in his prologue to *The Jew of Venice* (see **...and Nature Redressed**), Henrietta Maria Bowdler in her Preface to *The Family Shakespeare* is particularly suspicious of "foreign" (read "French") entertainments. The new British Shakespeare will mean, she hopes, that "the caprice of fashion may no longer seek for flimsy sentiment, false wit, and pernicious principles, in foreign dramatists" (p. x). In fact, she doesn't imagine Shakespeare on the stage at all. In a letter (now Folger MS Add 864) written in 1818, just after the expanded edition had appeared under her brother's

Loyie Elphinstone

THE
FAMILY
SHAKESPEARE.

IN FOUR VOLUMES.

VOL. I.

" The Stage might be made a perpetual Source of the moſt noble
" and uſeful Entertainment, were it under proper Regulations.''
ADDISON.

PRINTED BY
RICHARD CRUTTWELL, ST. JAMES's-STREET, BATH;
FOR
J. HATCHARD, BOOKSELLER TO HER MAJESTY,
NO. 190, PICCADILLY, LONDON.
1807.

Henrietta Maria Bowdler, ed., *The Family Shakespeare* (London: for J. Hatchard, 1807), title page. Twentieth-century politicians invented neither "family values" nor the censorship that would enforce them.

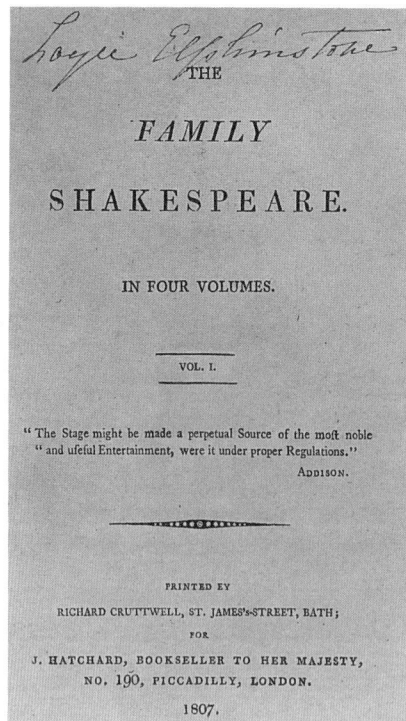

name, Henrietta Bowdler situates Shakespeare's plays cozily by the fire in the drawing room: shorn of "such passages as it w^d not be proper to read aloud," the new edition "will be the means of placing this charming Author in all Houses, & making him the companion of the winter evening in the country, to be read & admired as he deserves." Perhaps the ultimate attempt to rewrite Shakespeare's plays in the idiom of middle-class respectability was made by another brother-sister team, Charles and Mary Lamb, with their *Tales from Shakespear*, published the same year as the first edition of *The Family Shakespeare*.

Though most people might imagine Thomas Bowdler to have been a High Victorian Prude, he was very much a man of the late 18th century. Before setting up medical practice in London, he completed the Grand Tour that was *de rigueur* for 18th-century gentlemen. In the course of those travels he was received by Sir William Hamilton (1730–1803), British envoy in Naples, whom Bowdler thanks for his hospitality in a letter from London, dated 1 June 1781 (now Folger MS Y.c.248 [1]). Bowdler is even more grateful to Hamilton for having helped him get elected a fellow of The Royal Society. It was just two years ago today, Bowdler notes in the postscript, "that I had the pleasure of accompanying you in your curious Expedition across the running lava." The male protagonist in Susan Sontag's novel *The Volcano Lover* (1992), Hamilton is in many respects a highly unlikely correspondent for the editor of *The Family Shakespeare*. A year after he received

DOONESBURY BY G. B. TRUDEAU

LET'S PAUSE NOW FOR STATION IDENTIFICATION.

UM...CAN EVERYONE SEE THAT OKAY?

GOOD EVENING AND WELCOME TO CHANNEL Z, THE ADULT LATE-NIGHT CABLE STATION.

TONIGHT ON "CENSORED CLASSICS," WE BRING YOU AN EXCERPT FROM THE TORRID ORCHARD SCENE FROM ACT III OF SHAKESPEARE'S "ROMEO AND JULIET."

THE EXCERPT IS JUST ONE OF THE 320 LINES THAT HAVE BEEN EXPUNGED FROM THE WIDELY USED HIGH SCHOOL TEXT, "ADVENTURES IN READING."

PARENTS BE FOREWARNED. THE SCENE YOU ARE ABOUT TO SEE IS UNEXPURGATED, AND MAY BE DEEMED TOO INTENSE FOR TEENAGED VIEWERS. PARENTAL DISCRETION IS ADVISED.

"LOVERS CAN SEE TO DO THEIR AMOROUS RITES BY THEIR OWN BEAUTIES; OR IF LOVE BE BLIND, IT BEST AGREES WITH NIGHT."

OKAY, THAT'S ENOUGH EXCITEMENT FOR ONE NIGHT! CALL THE KIDS BACK IN.

G. B. Trudeau, Doonesbury cartoon on censorship of *Romeo and Juliet* (31 March 1985). Reproduced courtesy of G. B. Trudeau and the Universal Press Syndicate. When Doonesbury came to Verona in 1985, the result was a change in editorial policy on the part of at least one textbook publisher.

Bowdler's letter, Hamilton, ever the enthusiast for classical civilization, discovered in the province of Abruzzo a fully operational pagan fertility cult, which he gleefully described in letters to his friends. Hamilton and "The Cult of Priapus" remained a standing joke, rather ironically so when Hamilton's second wife, Emma, became Horatio Nelson's mistress. With respect to antiquity, Hamilton and Bowdler headed off in different directions. From rewriting Shakespeare, Bowdler moved on to rewriting history. At the time of his death he was attempting to bowdlerize Gibbon's *Decline and Fall of the Roman Empire*—no easy task, one would think, especially with the later emperors.

The spirit of Thomas Bowdler lives on in American high school textbooks. There was a time when *Julius Caesar* (recommended by its comparative brevity) introduced high school sophomores to Shakespeare. When educators decided that a play with adolescent protagonists might be more appealing, they had to contend not only with "open arse" but with scores of other bawdy bits. The usual solution has been simply to drop the offending lines, with nary a footnote to indicate their absence. The result not only honors "family values"; it makes for a shorter play that puts fewer demands on a student's attention span.

Forgery: Flattery or Fraud?

Shortly after Samuel Ireland

(d. 1800) returned from his "picturesque" tour to Warwickshire in 1793 (see **Nature Dressed...**), his son William Henry (1777–1835) began to bring home, one by one, Shakespearean documents of the very sort that had eluded the elder Ireland in Stratford. Among them were personal letters in Shakespeare's own handwriting and drafts of *Hamlet* and *Lear*, not to mention a hitherto unknown play called *Vortigern*. The documents belonged, William Henry said, to a mysterious "Mr. H," who had found them in an old chest. Reassembled in Samuel Ireland's house at Number 8 Norfolk Street in the Strand, the precious documents attracted a series of distinguished visitors, including James Boswell, who downed a tumbler of warm brandy and water, fell to his knees, and exclaimed, "I now kiss the invaluable relics of our bard: and thanks to God that I have lived to see them!" Not every Londoner was so enthusiastic, as John Nixon's "The Oaken Chest" (1797) makes clear.

Among the documents that young William Henry brought home was a fan letter from Queen Elizabeth, sent directly to "Master William Shakspeare atte the Globe bye Thames":

> Wee didde receive youre prettye Verses good Masterre William through the hands off our Lorde Chamberlayne ande wee doe Complemente thee onne theyre greate excellence Wee shalle departe fromme Londonne toe Hamptowne forre the holydayes where wee Shalle expecte thee withe thye beste Actorres thatte thou mayste playe before ourselfe toe amuse usse bee notte slowe butte comme toe usse bye Tuesdaye nexte asse the lorde Leicesterre wille bee withe usse
>
> Elizabeth R

The grateful playwright noted in his own hand: "Thys Letterre I dydde receyve fromme mye moste gracyouse Ladye Elyzabethe ande I doe requeste itte maye bee kepte withe alle care possyble. [signed] Wm Shakspeare." That "the Globe by Thames" was not built until ten years after the death of "the lorde Leicesterre" seems not to have bothered either the recipient or the postman.

The OakenChest er
the Gold Mines of Ireland a Farce,
"the Earth hath Bubbles as the Water has & these are them. Shakspere

John Nixon (d. 1818), "The Oaken Chest or The Gold Mines of Ireland, a Farce," colored engraving (1797). Boswell worshiped; others laughed.

So that all of society might see the Shakespearean documents that his son William Henry had brought to light, Samuel Ireland gathered subscriptions (at four guineas apiece, according to Nixon's print "The Oaken Chest") for a folio volume that would reproduce all of the documents in facsimile, along with full transcriptions. In the Folger collection is a sumptuously bound copy of *Miscellaneous Papers and Legal Instruments under the Hand and Seal of William Shakspeare . . . from the Original MSS. in the Possession of Samuel Ireland, of Norfolk Street* (London, 1796) that was intended, according to a note in William Henry's hand, for "the supposed original Possessor of the MSS." The mysterious "Mr. H," who refused to come forward but who communicated through William Henry his desire that the papers be published, never received this copy, for good reason. He didn't exist. William Henry had made him up, as he confessed when Edmund Malone finally stepped forward in *An Inquiry into the Authenticity of Certain Miscellaneous Papers and Legal Instruments . . .* (1796) and exposed all the documents as forgeries. Malone's move came just in time. *Vortigern* was just about to open at Drury Lane.

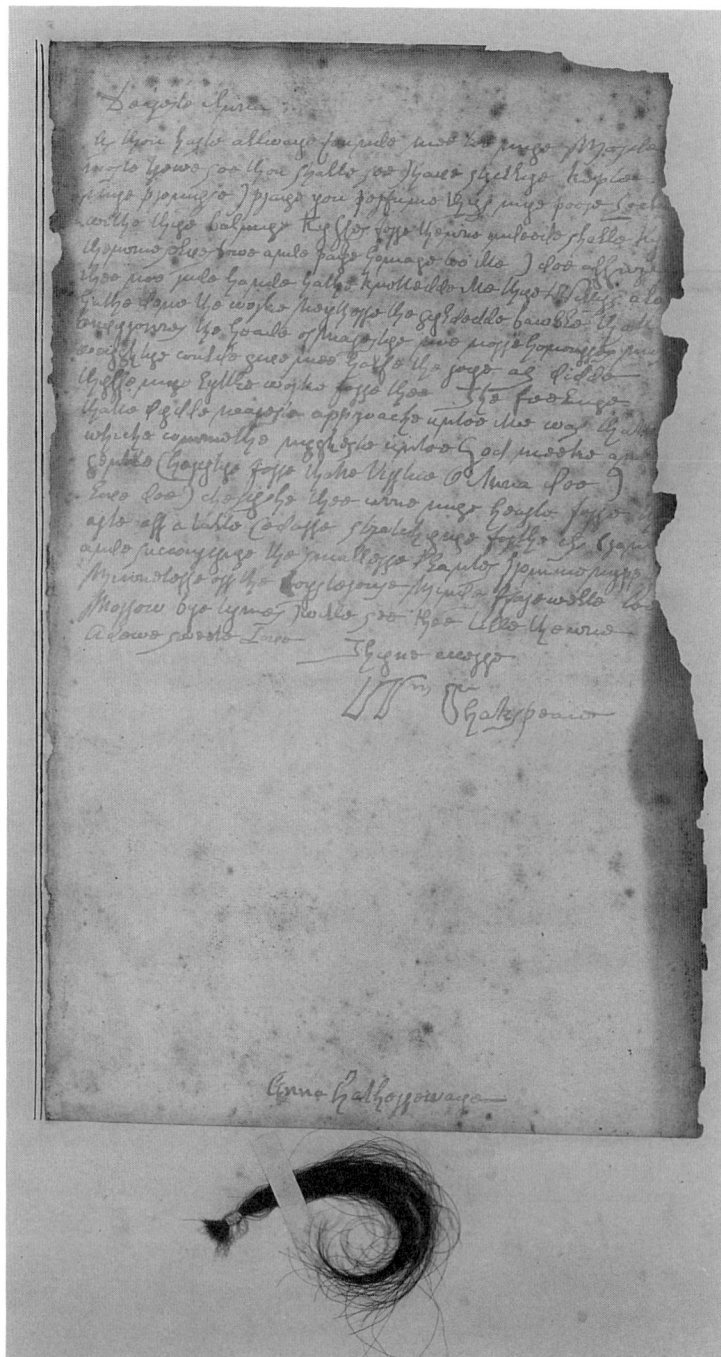

Supposed letter from William Shakespeare to Anne Hathaway (Folger MS W.b.496, fol. 93). If Nixon's "The Oaken Chest" is to be believed, the tuft of hair affixed to the manuscript is only part of the prodigious knot that visitors could see at Number 8 Norfolk Street.

Ten years after Malone had uncovered the fraud, William Henry Ireland published a book of *Confessions* (1806) in which he explained how he produced the forgeries—and why. He did it all to please his aloof and condescending father. The Folger owns a specially bound volume (Folger MS W.b.496) that interleaves pages of *Miscellaneous Papers* (1796) and *Confessions* (1806) with William Henry's original forgeries, including the fan letter from Queen Elizabeth (fol. 105) and an effusive letter from William Shakespeare to "Anna Hatherreweye" (fol. 93). "Willy" has honored a promise by enclosing a lock of his hair.

Dearesste Anna

As thou haste alwaye founde mee toe mye Worde moste trewe soe thou shalt see I have stryctlye kepte mye promyse I praye you perfume thys mye poore Locke with thye balmye Kysses forre thenne indeede shalle Kynges themmeselves bowe ande paye homage toe itte I doe assure thee no rude hande hathe knottedde itte thye Willys alone hathe done the worke Neytherre the gyldedde bawble thatte envyronnes the heade of Majestye noe norre honourres moste weyghtye wulde give mee halfe the joye as didde thysse mye lyttle worke forre thee The feelinge thatte dydde neareste approache untoe itte was thatte whiche commethe nygheste untoe Gode meeke and Gentle Charytye forre thatte Virrtue O Anna doe I love doe I cheryshe thee inne mye hearte forre thou arte ass a talle Cedarre stretchynge forthe its branches ande succourynge the smallere Plants fromme nyppynge Winneterre orr the boysterouse Wyndes Farewelle toe Morrow by tymes I wille see thee tille thenne Adewe sweete Love

Thyne everre
Wm Shakspeare

Fraud with respect to Shakespeare began long before the 18th century, and continued long after. When the printers Thomas Pavier and William Jaggard tried to issue a collected edition of some of Shakespeare's scripts in 1619, the Lord Chamberlain personally intervened to stop them, presumably to prevent them from scooping the First Folio, which appeared four years later. To get around the Lord Chamberlain's order, Pavier falsified the publication date on a reprint of *The First Part of the True & Honorable History, of the Life of Sir John Old-castle . . .* (London: for T.P., 1600)—and added "Written by William Shakespeare" to the title page, for good measure. Shakespeare, dead for three years, had nothing to do with the whole affair. He had not even written the play. It was the box-office caché of Shakespeare's Falstaff, based on the historical Sir John Oldcastle and originally so named in Shakespeare's *Henry IV* plays, that had prompted Philip Henslowe to commission the two parts of *Sir John Oldcastle* for his own company, a rival to Shakespeare's, in 1599. As payments recorded in Henslowe's diary make clear, the actual authors of the play were Anthony Munday, Michael Drayton, Robert Wilson, and Richard Hathaway.

The appearance of the First Folio in 1623 failed to settle what William Shakespeare had really written and what he had not. At

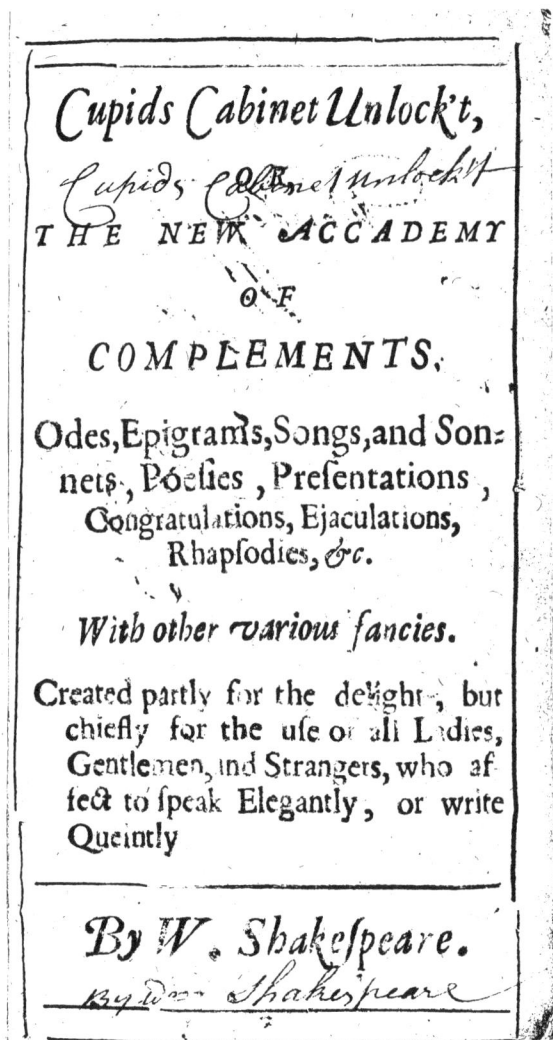

Cupids Cabinet Unlock't,

THE NEW ACCADEMY OF

COMPLEMENTS.

Odes, Epigrams, Songs, and Sonnets, Posies, Presentations, Congratulations, Ejaculations, Rhapsodies, &c.

With other various fancies.

Created partly for the delight, but chiefly for the use of all Ladies, Gentlemen, and Strangers, who affect to speak Elegantly, or write Queintly

By W. Shakespeare.

Cupid's Cabinet Unlock't (n.p., n.d. [before 1700]), title page. An early owner of the Folger copy, William Milner, has taken the title page's advice and appropriated the works as his own by transcribing the title and Shakespeare's name in his own hand and by writing out his own first-person verses on the reverse of the title page. What Milner has done graphically critics have done figuratively.

least three scripts in which Shakespeare had a hand (or so modern scholarship indicates) were left out of the First Folio: *Pericles, The Two Noble Kinsmen,* and *Sir Thomas More.* Contemporaries associate Shakespeare's name with two other plays that are now presumed to be lost: *Love's Labors Won* and *Cardenio.* To complicate matters further, the Third Folio (1663) adds not only *Pericles* but six other plays that have come to be known as "the Shakespeare Apocrypha." In such a state of affairs, William Henry Ireland's "discovery" of *Vortigern* is less farfetched than it might at first seem. The fact that the First Folio is limited to Shakespeare's playscripts—none of his nondramatic poems is included—made it all the easier for 17th-century anthologists to attribute to William Shakespeare any stray poem that struck them. Witness *Cupid's Cabinet Unlock't* (n.p., n.d. [before 1700]), which despite the appearance of "W. Shakespeare" on the title page contains not a single line now attributed to William Shakespeare. Printed in a size handy for pockets, *Cupid's Cabinet Unlock't* is a "how-to" book with ready-made verses for every occasion (when presenting a lady with a new pair of gloves, for example), as well as poesies for inscribing inside rings.

William Milner's use of Shakespeare to further his amorous career in the early 18th century seems charmingly innocent compared to John Payne Collier's use of Shakespeare to further his scholarly career a hundred years or so later. Significantly, perhaps, the first old book that Collier acquired was a copy of the Shakespeare Third Folio, with its "expanded" canon. Having established a scholarly reputation with his first book, *The History of English Dramatic Poetry to the Time of Shakespeare . . .* (1831), Collier gained access to genuine 16th- and 17th-century papers in private libraries and proceeded to add to his benefactors' collections by inserting forged documents full of all sorts of interesting facts about William Shakespeare's professional career. These undiscovered documents Collier then published with a scholarly reticence that duped most of his contemporaries—until chemical and paleographical analysis of the emendations he had added to a copy of the Second Folio (presumably from lost Shakespearean manuscripts) called into question all his other "discoveries." One of Collier's specialties as a forger was ballads. His handiwork can be witnessed in a commonplace book dating to 1630–40 now in the Folger (MS V.a.339). Because the original 17th-century owner of this manuscript volume had organized the poems he entered under subject headings, there were plenty of blank pages scattered throughout the volume when Collier acquired it. On these blank leaves Collier entered, in a fake secretary hand, eighty-three ballads that he then claimed as discoveries. Some of the ballads came from printed sources; others Collier made up himself. Among the latter is this poem "Against the newe Playhouses"—an attack on the very institution that provided Collier with his scholarly reputation:

> The fire that fro[m] heaven fell
> On Sodom and Gomarh of olde
> Upon this Towne may fall as well
> ffor all our vices manifolde
> The nomber great may not be tolde
> But one there is past all the rest
> That God and Christ must sure detest[.]
>   (fol. 170ᵛ)

Shakespeare Sacrificed

When the upstart crow of the 16th century became canonized as the British National Poet in the 18th century, wily merchants were just as eager as witty mockers to do the occasion justice. Both knew a good thing when they saw it. The critical premises that secured Shakespeare his place of prominence were supplied by Samuel Johnson in the Preface to his edition of Shakespeare's plays (London: J. and R. Tonson, 1765):

> Nothing can please many, and please long, but just representations of general nature. Particular manners can be known to few, and therefore few only can judge how nearly they are copied. The irregular combinations of fanciful invention may delight a-while by that novelty of which the common satiety of life sends us all in quest; but the pleasures of sudden wonder are soon exhausted; and the mind can only repose on the stability of truth.
>
> Shakespeare is, above all writers, at least above all modern writers, the poet of nature, the poet that holds up to his readers a faithful mirrour of manners and of life. His characters are not modified by the customs of particular places, unpractised by the rest of the world; by the peculiarities of studies or professions, which can operate but upon small numbers; or by the accidents of transient fashions or temporary opinions: they are the genuine progeny of common humanity, such as the world will always supply, and observation will always find. His persons act and speak by the influence of those general passions and principles by which all minds are agitated and the whole system of life is continued in motion. In the writings of other poets a character is too often an individual; in those of *Shakespeare* it is commonly a species.
>
> (*Plays*, Vol. 1, sigs. A2^v–A3)

What this amounts to is nothing short of a redefinition of "Nature." The pastoral trappings amid which Shakespeare had languished since Jonson and Milton are replaced here by something more intellectually respectable. Another sign of the times in Johnson's edition was the fine leather binding that recommended such multi-volume editions of Shakespeare's plays to middle-class bookshelves.

Chelsea Gold Anchor porcelain, Standing statue of Shakespeare (1758–69). When a standing statue of Shakespeare, after a design by William Kent (1684–1748), finally joined the august company assembled in Poet's Corner of Westminster Abbey in 1741, commercial copies began to appear in all sorts of media and in all sorts of sizes. (A life-size copy, now lost, is the earliest recorded image of Shakespeare in North America.) The elegiac mood of the original statue (in which Shakespeare gestures toward a scroll inscribed "The Cloud Capt Towers, the gorgeous palaces . . .") gives way in this porcelain miniature to a colorful exuberance that is more at home on a mantlepiece than in an abbey. By the middle of the 18th century Shakespeare had been turned into a collectible.

In the new adulation of Shakespeare, an apogee of sorts was reached when actor/impresario David Garrick and other London sponsors arranged a "Stratford Jubilee" celebration for September 1769. A grand procession of Shakespeare's characters, fireworks, music, dancing, horseracing, and speechifying all helped to turn Stratford-upon-Avon into the pilgrims' shrine it remains today. Relics of the newly canonized cultural saint were to be had in the form of objects made from the wood of a mulberry tree Shakespeare was supposed to have planted in the grounds of New Place. (The tree, not to mention New Place itself, was no longer to be seen by 1769, thanks to the ministrations of the Reverend Francis Gastrell, who bought New Place in 1753, chopped down the tree to keep away curiosity-seekers, and later razed the entire building when town officials insisted he pay full property taxes on a dwelling he lived in only part of the time.) Festivities in 1769 included this jovial piece by Charles Dibdin, sung by David Garrick as he drank from a vessel made from the sacred wood:

> Behold this fair goblet, 'twas carv'd from the tree,
> Which, O my sweet Shakespeare, was planted by thee!
> As a relic I kiss it, and bow at the shrine,
> What comes from thy hand must be ever divine.

(Whether or not Garrick broke into blank verse after downing the contents is not recorded.) Some of the Folger Library's least-known treasures include a ceramic cup (c. 1750) showing "Shakespeare's mulberry tree" and a rolling pin said to have been made from the same by Thomas Sharp (d. 1799), a Stratford watchmaker who bought the wood of the felled tree and proceeded to turn out enough curios to rival relics of the True Cross. Back at Drury Lane, where some of Garrick's greatest triumphs were in roles from Shakespeare, the grand pageant that he had designed for Stratford ran for ninety performances. Less pomp, and rather more sordid circumstance, are offered by the backstage drawings that Thomas Rowlandson (1756–1827) and Georg Emanuel Opiz (1775–1827) produced of Shakespeare's plays in performance.

Garrick was hardly alone in capitalizing on Shakespeare. John Boydell (1719–1804) found another way to celebrate Britain's national poet and, at the same time, to secure a European reputation for British history painting, not to mention a tidy profit for himself. Already successful as a print publisher and dealer, Boydell issued a prospectus for his scheme in 1786. He proposed to commission major British artists to illustrate scenes from all of Shakespeare's plays, to construct a gallery in which to display their works, to set engravers to work on reproducing the paintings, and to publish two sets of engravings, one a luxurious folio edition of large plates and the other a set of smaller plates designed to illustrate a lavish new edition of Shakespeare's plays.

In establishing a reputation for British history painting, John Boydell and his nephew and business partner Josiah Boydell (1752–1817) may have been fulfilling Sir Joshua Reynolds's vision of literary and historical subjects as the highest of the visual arts, but some people knew a scam when they saw one. When John Boydell turned down James Gillray's application to engrave one of the plates, Gillray responded with "Shakespeare-Sacrificed" (1789). Boydell, wearing his robes as an alderman of London, stands within a magic circle as he burns Shakespeare's works

Unknown 18th-century artist, the Reverend Francis Gastrell (active 1756–1768), portrait miniature, lent by the Shakespeare Birthplace Trust. Not everyone shared in the 18th-century cult of The National Poet. Having bought New Place, the house in Stratford to which Shakespeare retired, the Reverend Gastrell first chopped down a mulberry tree that Shakespeare was said to have planted, and then pulled down the house itself in a dispute over property taxes. He left Stratford, it is said, "amid the curses and execrations of the populace."

Thomas Rowlandson (1756–1827), *Macbeth* in performance, pen and ink and watercolor on paper. The new cult of Shakespeare as Universal Genius (read "British Genius") invited less lofty views.

before Avarice, grinning atop an altar formed by a fat volume of the subscribers to Boydell's scheme. Prominent among the creatures being conjured in the sacrifice is Fuseli's Bottom.

Whatever it may have done for the reputations of Shakespeare and of British history painting, Boydell's enterprise spelled financial trouble for himself. In April 1791 a vandal slashed some of the paintings. In another satiric acquatint, "The Monster Broke Loose" (1791), Gillray proposed that it was Boydell himself who did the slashing for the sake of publicity. Admission fees to the gallery in Pall Mall were not, however, the real money-making part of the venture. Boydell, after all, was a print publisher. He knew his market. What he didn't know is how far costs would outstrip subscriptions and how many delays there would be in completing the project. By the time the folio came out in 1803, Boydell could save his publishing business only by organizing a lottery in which the gallery and its contents were the prize. In 1805 the gallery closed, and its contents were auctioned off one by one. Twelve of the paintings, including Romney's *The Infant Shakespeare, Attended by Nature and the Passions*, eventually found their way into the collections of the Folger Library.

Henry Fuseli (1741–1825), *A Midsummer Night's Dream, Act 4, Scene 1*, engraved by Peter Simon, Plate 20 in *A Collection of Prints from Pictures Painted for the Purpose of Illustrating the Dramatic Works of Shakespeare by the Artists of Great Britain* (London: John and Josiah Boydell, 1803). When the Boydells' gallery opened at 52 Pall Mall in 1789, Henry Fuseli's illustration of Bottom's tryst with Titania was one of the 34 pictures on view.

SHAKSPEARE,
Midsummer Nights Dream.
ACT IV, SCENE I.

James Gillray (1757–1815),
"Shakespeare-Sacrificed; or
The Offering to Avarice,"
acquatint (1789). To one observor
at least, Boydell's version of *A
Midsummer Night's Dream* looked
more like a lurid nightmare.

Ungenial Geniuses

Ben Jonson (see **Nature Dressed…**)

is only the first in a long line of writers famous enough in their own right who have nonetheless begrudged Shakespeare the adulation he seems to have inspired on all sides. Grounds for condescension have sometimes been high-mindedly philosophical, sometimes politically entrenched, but *never* basely green.

Even if they had not been written in English, Shakespeare's decidedly *un*classical plays would have given an enlightened French intellectual little reason to smile. Voltaire's philosophical premises were such that, if Shakespeare had not existed, Voltaire would have had to invent him. In his early volume of pronounce-ments on British culture, translated as *Letters Concerning the English Nation* (London: C. Davis and A. Lyon, 1733), the Frenchman finds in Shakespeare a handy target for his altogether logical Anglophobia:

> *Shakespear* boasted a strong, fruitful Genius: He was natural and sublime, but had not so much as a single Spark of good Taste, or knew one Rule of the Drama. I will now hazard a random, but, at the same Time, true Reflection, which is, that the great Merit of this Dramatic Poet has been the Ruin of the *English* Stage.
>
> (pp. 166–167)

Vive, as a more recent French philosopher would put it, *la différance*. (See Derrida *infra* **Deconstructors**.)

A man who could write a book no less sweeping than *War and Peace* (1863–69) and then denounce his own work in a book no less ambitious than *What is Art?* (1898) would certainly feel no hesitation about denouncing the work of someone else, even William Shakespeare. "I remember the astonishment I felt when I first read Shakespeare," Tolstoi confesses.

> I expected to receive a powerful esthetic pleasure, but having read, one after the other, works regarded as his best: "King Lear," "Romeo and Juliet," "Hamlet," and "Macbeth," not only did I feel no delight, but I felt an irresistible repulsion and tedium, and doubted as to whether I was senseless in feeling works regarded as the summit of perfection by the whole of the civilized world to be trivial and positively bad, or

Pierre Gabriel Langlois (1754–1810) after Maurice Quentin de La Tour (1704–1788), portrait of François Marie Arouet de Voltaire (1694–1778), engraving. The smile on this man's face is the smile of reason.

whether the significance which this civilized world attributes to the works of Shakespeare was itself senseless.

After that forthright statement on page 4, the rest of *Tolstoy on Shakespeare*, trans. V. Tchertkoff and I. F. M. (New York and London: Funk and Wagnalls, 1906), is devoted to judging Shakespeare's plays against the criteria of understandability and moral commitment enunciated in *What Is Art?* Shakespeare's plays do not come off well. A particularly memorable chapter catalogs the artistic and psychological absurdities of *King Lear*.

Tolstoy on Shakespeare was published with an Afterword by George Bernard Shaw, who by 1906 was already famous for his own antipathy to the Bard. Take, for example, this diatribe, written in 1896:

> There are moments when one asks despairingly why our stage should ever have been cursed with this "immortal" pilferer of other men's stories and ideas, with his monstrous rhetorical fustian, his unbearable platitudes, his pretentious reduction of the subtlest problems of life to commonplaces against which a Polytechnic debating club would revolt, his incredible unsuggestiveness, his sententious combination of ready reflection with complete intellectual sterility, and his consequent incapacity for getting out of the depth of even the most ignorant audience, except when he solemnly says something so transcendently platitudinous that his more humble-minded

G.B. SHAW "Cutting" SHAKESPEARE IN HADES.

G.B.S. RESERVED. GRID.

Kyd

Joseph Clayton Clarke ("Kyd") (active 1883–1894), "G. B. Shaw 'Cutting' Shakespeare in Hades," watercolor and ink on paper. For the word "Bardolatry" we can thank George Bernard Shaw (1856–1950). After years of sparring with Shakespeare in his reviews of the London stage, Shaw in the Preface to *Three Plays for Puritans* (1906) finally hit upon just the right term for the public's uncritical enthusiasm for Shakespeare—an enthusiasm inspired, in Shaw's view, not by direct knowledge of the plays but by the "spurious and silly" productions that had held the stage from the 18th century until Shaw's own time (p. lvi).

hearers cannot bring themselves to believe that so great a man really meant to talk like their grandmothers. With the single exception of Homer, there is no eminent writer, not even Sir Walter Scott, whom I can despise so entirely as I despise Shakespeare when I measure my mind against his.

The occasion for this particular exercise in "Blaming the Bard" was a review of a production of *Cymbeline* ("for the most part stagey trash of the lowest melodramatic order") reprinted in Shaw's collected *Dramatic Opinions and Essays* (London: Constable, 1907), pp. 51–52.

Shaw will grant Shakespeare the gift of telling a good story, power over language, humor, and a sense of idiosyncratic character, not to mention the "vital energy" that distinguishes "the man of genius." What Shakespeare lacks is rigor as a thinker, and for that Shaw blames the stage itself. In *The Dark Lady of the Sonnets*

Mrs. Patrick Campbell as Ophelia in 1897, photograph. Whatever G.B.S. may have thought—about Shakespeare or about strong male speakers—his friend Mrs. Patrick Campbell (1865–1940) scored numerous successes as Shakespeare's heroines.

(London: Constable, 1910), an "interlude" Shaw wrote in support of the campaign to build a national theater for (of all things) performing Shakespeare's plays, Shaw has Shakespeare confess to Queen Elizabeth that some of his most popular plays were pot-boilers: "I have writ these to save my friends from penury, yet shewing my scorn for such follies and for them that praise them by calling the one As You Like It, meaning that it is not as *I* like it, and the other Much Ado About Nothing, as it truly is" (p. 13). All the more reason that Queen Elizabeth should endow a theater for performing truly serious plays like *Lear*, *Macbeth*, and *Hamlet*, plays in which, as Shaw says in the Preface,

> Burbage's power and popularity as an actor enabled Shakespear to free himself from the tyranny of the box office, and to express himself more freely in plays consisting largely of monologue to be spoken by a great actor from whom the public would stand a good deal.[6]

6. G. B. Shaw, *Misalliance, The Dark Lady of the Sonnets, and Fanny's First Play* (London: Constable, 1914), p. 131. The Folger Library's copy of *The Dark Lady of the Sonnets* (London: Constable, 1910), bears the printed subtitle "Rough Proof-Unpublished" and does not include the defensive preface Shaw published four years later.

That is to say, Shakespeare's best plays are just like the ones Shaw himself wrote.

"What in Hell Did He Ever Do for Denver?"

The remark made by silver-rich Horace Tabor when he saw that Shakespeare had been given pride of place on the proscenium arch of the Grand Opera House that Tabor himself was paying for typifies American ambivalence about Shakespeare—an ambivalence that ranges somewhere between awe-struck and "Aw shucks." The awe-struck side showed up early.

William Heath's print "The Rival Richards, or Sheakspear in Danger" (1814) was designed to satirize the rivalry of Edmund Kean (1787–1833), left, and Charles Mayne Young (1777–1856), right, who played the role of Richard III in a fustian style that contrasted with Kean's comparative naturalism. An early annotator of the Folger's copy of the print has updated the occasion to the much more famous rivalry between Kean and Junius Brutus Booth, who copied Kean's style so well that he posed a serious threat to Kean's reign over the London stage. Kean's first strategy when Booth appeared on the scene in 1817 was to sign Booth up as an actor at his own theater, Drury Lane, assuring that the young actor from the provinces would always play secondary roles to Kean's leads. When Booth signed a contract at the rival house, Covent Garden, London audiences were treated to rival productions of *Richard III*—and to several nights of rioting by partisans of the rival actors. After losing his hold on the public imagination, Booth sailed off to America, where his first performance—at Richmond, Virginia, on 6 July 1821—was in the role of Richard III. Booth went on to a hugely successful American career and founded a dynasty of American actors, including John Wilkes Booth (1838–1865), whose last *official* appearance onstage occurred in Washington, on 18 March 1865. The venue was Ford's Theater. The play was called *The Apostate*. In the same house, less than one month later, John Wilkes Booth enacted a tragedy of his own devising.

William Heath (1795–1840), "The Rival Richards, or Sheakspear in Danger" (1814), colored engraving. An early annotator has identified the Richard on the left with Junius Brutus Booth (1796–1852), the actor who brought big-time Shakespeare to America.

Adulation has been only part of America's response to Shakespeare. Solemnity on the one hand has inspired satire on the other. Take, for example, Mark Twain. In the long run the most famous Shakespearean actors in America may not be Junius Brutus Booth and Sir Laurence Olivier but the duke and the dolphin in *Huckleberry Finn* (1885). The originals for this fictional pair are set in place in two passages Twain wrote for *Life on the Mississippi* (1883) but decided were too unflattering to print. Having looked over foreign travelers' accounts of what America was like in the 1830s, Twain records two memorable performances of *Hamlet* in Pittsburgh:

> There was no actual Buffalo, or Cleveland, or Chicago, when the earlier tourists went browsing through the land, and not enough of a Pittsburgh to hang more than this comment on— by a sorely disgusted English eye-witness: that an English dramatic troupe played Hamlet there one night, in the regulation way, and played a burlesque of it the next night; but they didn't *tell* the audience it was a burlesque; so the women-folk went on crying whilst the roaring, gigantic Ophelia cavorted hither and thither, scattering her carrots and cabbages around, in lieu of rosemary and rue; but they, and the men, too, complained next day, that the performance, taken by and large, was bad—yes, and here and there extravagant, even![7]

7. This, along with other passages that were cut from the original edition of *Life on the Mississippi*, is restored in the Penguin edition (New York: Penguin, 1984), pp. 291–293.

HAMLET'S SOLILOQUY.

Mark Twain, *Adventures of Huckleberry Finn* (New York: Charles L. Webster and Co., 1885), p. 178, collection of Prof. John Hirsh, Georgetown University. "To be, or not to be; that is the bare bodkin/ That makes calamity of so long life . . .": the duke's performance as Hamlet in small-town Arkansas not only satirizes the florid style of Sir Henry Irving (1838–1905), the reigning Shakespearean actor of Twain's day; it recalls actual performances in frontier America of fifty years before.

Thomas Nast (1840–1903), Study for *The Immortal Light of Genius* (1895), oil on paper laid down on canvas. It was over a post-theater supper at the Beefsteak Club in London that Sir Henry Irving proposed to Nast the idea for a serious painting about Shakespeare. *The Immortal Light of Genius*, finished on Shakespeare's birthday, 23 April 1896, was the result.

If it was Shakespeare, it was Culture. If it was Culture, it had to be solemn. American assumptions that Culture is one thing and entertainment something else again persist on the cover of *Esquire* magazine for March 1993: "Shakespeare's Dead!/ Roseanne's Syndicated!"

American indecision about just what to *do* with Shakespeare—worship him as a cultural hero or treat him as "one of us"—is registered graphically in the works of Thomas Nast. Creator of the Democratic donkey and the Republican elephant, Nast often worked images and speeches from Shakespeare into the more than 3000 political cartoons he drew for *Harper's Weekly* between 1862 and 1885. Toward the end of his life he produced a more solemn tribute to Shakespeare. Nast's preparatory oil sketch for *The Immortal Light of Genius* (the original has been destroyed) shows a

THOS. NAST

IN HIS

ARTISTIC ENTERTAINMENT

Drawing in Black and White and Painting in OIL Colors

IN PRESENCE OF THE AUDIENCE.

News Print, Denver.

Advertisement for "Thos. Nast in His Artistic Entertainment Drawing in Black and White and Painting in OIL Colors in Presence of the Audience" (probably 1887). Nast's more usual metier is suggested by this advertisement for one of the illustrated lectures that took the famous cartoonist on several tours all over the United States and left him quite a wealthy man. Since it was printed in Denver, this particular poster probably dates from 1887, when Nast came west to inspect a mine in which he had invested. His discovery that the mine was worthless left him quite a less wealthy man, and he set out on the lecture trail once again.

distinctively 19th-century fusion of the real and the surreal. A bust of Shakespeare stands, just as late 19th-century visitors to Stratford would have seen it, in the room in which Shakespeare is said to have been born. What an illustrator for *Harper's Weekly* would not have seen is the unearthly inner light that radiates from the bust, not to mention the figures of Comedy and Tragedy that advance to crown it. *"Shakespeare in America"*: British artist Tom Phillips (b. 1937) hit upon just the right device for visualizing the theme of the 1976 International Shakespeare Congress in Washington. Phillips's commemorative poster takes the icon of Shakespeare's likeness from the First Folio, turns it by degrees into a comic strip, and juxtaposes it with the titles of American take-offs ("Kiss Me Kate," "The Boys from Syracuse," "West Side Story") scrawled on the Folio's table of contents like technicolored graffiti.

Sir Bernard Partridge (1861–1945), "Uncle Sam" stealing British masterpieces, pencil and ink on paper. Shakespeare immigrated to the United States in more lasting form once American businessmen had hit upon art collecting and book collecting as ways of giving a patina of old wealth to newly minted dollars. Not every new millionaire was as brusque as Horace Tabor. Since "Uncle Sam" in Sir Bernard Partridge's drawing has Gainsborough's *Blue Boy* under one arm and a First Folio of Shakespeare under the other, the pillager in this case is (thank goodness) probably Henry Huntington (1850–1927) and not Henry Clay Folger (1857–1930). Acting on an enthusiasm for Shakespeare that dated from his student days at Amherst College, Folger eventually bought seventy-nine copies of the First Folio, not to mention assorted fragments, making his collection of First Folios the largest one anywhere. For the most prized of these volumes, a presentation copy from the printer, Isaac Jaggard, to a friend, the price Folger paid in 1903 was £10,000— a sum approaching one million dollars in today's currency.

THE BLUE BOY
T. GAINSBOROUGH

SHAKESPEARE
FIRST FOLIO
1623

GOOD FREND, FOR JESUS' SAKE FORBEARE
TO DIGG THE DUST ENCLOASED HEARE:
BLESTE BE THE MAN THAT SPARES THES STONES,
AND CURST BE HE THAT MOVES MY BONES.

Bernard Partridge.

Egging on Bacon

Shakespeare's most intractable detractors are not the likes of Voltaire, Tolstoi, and Shaw, who at least concede that he existed, but the people who think "the Stratford man" couldn't possibly have written the plays ascribed to him. Snobbery about Shakespeare's learning ("he had little") and gossip about his thievery ("he made his reputation by pilfering other men's works") go back to *Greene's Groatsworth of Wit* (see **Eating Crow**), but it was an 18th-century academic, James Wilmot, who first pieced together the theory that the works ascribed to William Shakespeare had in fact been written by someone else, namely Francis Bacon. Wilmot's suspicions were first aroused when he retired from Trinity College, Oxford, took up the rectorship of a small parish near Stratford-upon-Avon, and began to search Warwickshire archives for information he could use in a projected new biography of Warwickshire's most famous son. All he turned up were oral legends about Shakespeare the butcher's son, a rogue who poached deer in his youth, went off to London to seek his fortune, never earned a single mention in letters and documents of the local gentry, and left in his will not a single surviving book or manuscript. Could this be the man who wrote some of the world's greatest literary works? From the social and economic perspective of the 1780s and 90s it seemed unlikely.

Wilmot's views remained unpublished during his lifetime. The mantle of chief prophet of the Baconian heresy falls instead on an American, Delia Bacon, who made it her life's work to prove that Shakespeare's plays had in fact been written by her famous namesake. In *The Philosophy of the Plays of Shakspere Unfolded* (Boston: Ticknor and Fields, 1857), Delia Bacon bolsters the academic snobbery of Robert Greene and James Wilmot with the trappings of science. In 675 densely written and tightly printed pages she argues that the works wrongly attributed to Shakespeare constitute the missing fourth part of Francis Bacon's *Great Instauration*, an illustration of the revolutionary principles Bacon sets forth in the *Novum Organum*.

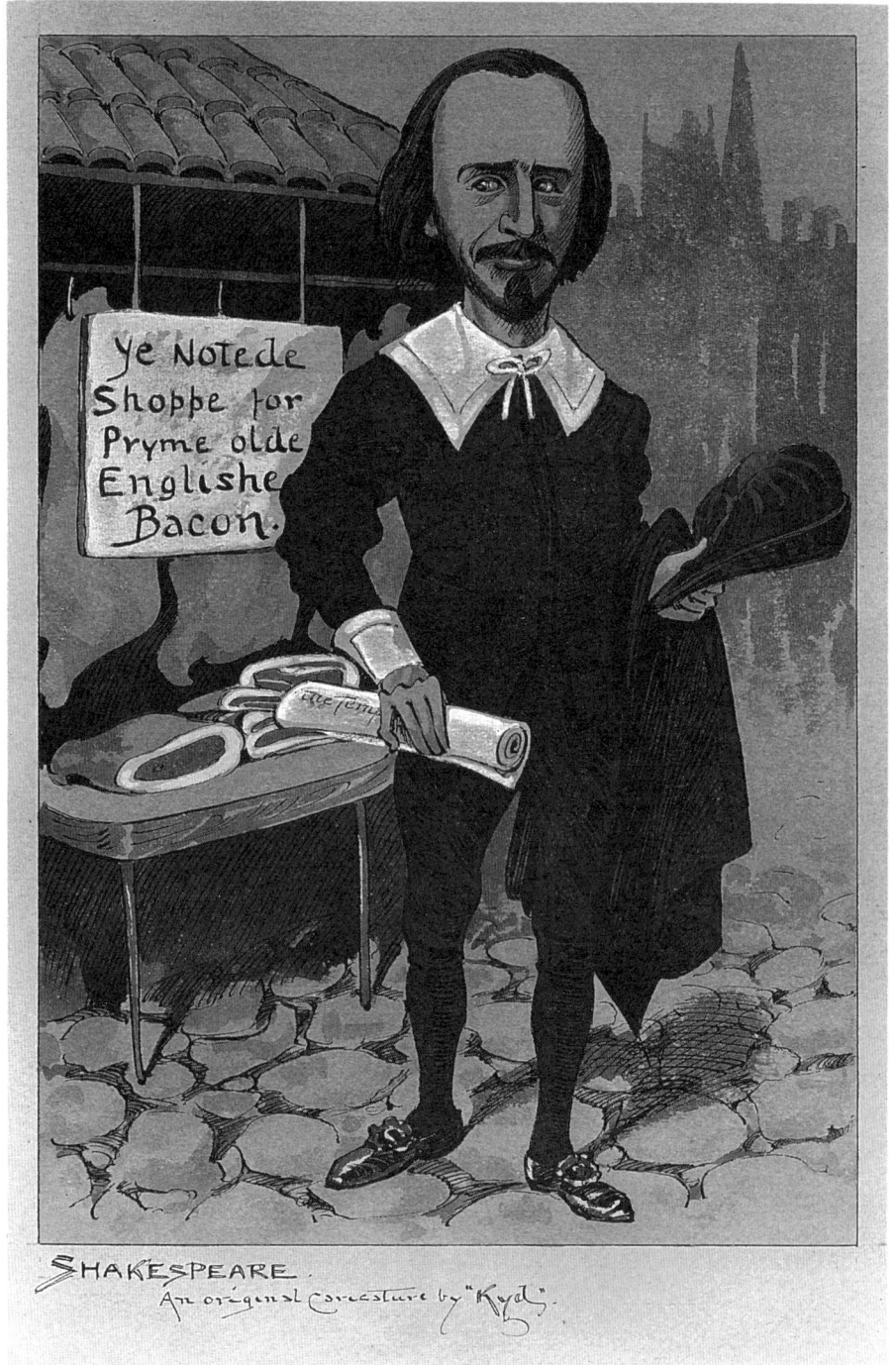

Joseph Clayton Clarke ("Kyd") (active 1883–1894), Shakespeare and Bacon, watercolor and ink on paper. In addition to writing Shakespeare's plays, Francis Bacon is supposed by some to have written a plan for world peace, a lost document that is possibly buried in Williamsburg, Virginia.

Delia Bacon (1811–1859), contemporary photograph. Carlyle laughed, but Hawthorne was kind.

Copyright 1888 by Theodore Bacon.

Very gratefully yours
Delia Bacon,

From a Daguerreotype taken in May 1853.

That Delia Bacon's work should be published by such a distinguished house as Ticknor and Fields and carry a preface by Nathaniel Hawthorne is a story in itself. Sailing to England in search of evidence for her thesis, Bacon failed to find anyone who took her seriously. Thomas Carlyle received her but laughed uncontrollably when she told him her mission. Finally she wrote in desperation to Hawthorne, the U. S. Consul in Liverpool. In that letter (now Folger MS Y.c.2599 no. 90) it takes her six densely written pages, and an appeal to heaven, to ask Hawthorne to look over her manuscript:

> If it were anything in the world but what it is,—a science,— a science that the world is waiting for, I could not do and suffer what I have done and suffered on its behalf. I ought not to hesitate at all to ask for all the help I need in it, for it is a work which the Providence of this world has imposed on me, and I have cast into its treasury not only all the living that I had, such as it was, but my life also.

Hawthorne's reply (now Folger MS Y.c.2599 no. 214) manages a gracious but guarded politeness. He promises to help her, but is careful to protect himself when it comes to Bacon's claims against the "old player" from Stratford:

> I would not be understood, my dear Miss Bacon, as professing to have faith in the correctness of your views. In fact, I know far too little of them to have any right to form an opinion; and as to the case of the 'old Player' (whom you grieve my heart by speaking of so contemptuously) you will have to rend him out of [me] by the roots, and by main force, if at all.

After meeting Bacon face to face a short time later, Hawthorne took compassion on her, helped her find a publisher, contributed a preface, and even subvented some of the costs of publication without Bacon's knowledge.

When *The Philosophy of the Plays of Shakspere Unfolded* drew hoots of derision instead of raptures of praise, Delia Bacon entered into a physical and mental decline that has made her the patron saint of the Baconian cause. Aside from the predictable dismissals of Shakespeare scholars and graphic ridicule by cartoonists like "Kyd," there was the personal indignation felt by ordinary people who happened to be Shakespearean enthusiasts, people like J. Woods Poinier Jr. of New York City, who assembled a scrapbook of Shakespeareana, now in the collections of the Folger, between 1872 and 1876. Pasted into Poinier's scrapbook is a cartoon, clipped from a magazine in October 1874, that shows the distraught ghost of Shakespeare observing laurel wreaths being laid on a bust of Bacon. "The Spirit of Shakespeare" is captioned to say, "He who steals my purse steals trash, but he who takes from me my good name, etc." The spirit in which Poinier read the cartoon is indicated by the inscription he made on page one of his scrapbook:

> This collection of notices of The World's Poet is made by the Collector out of his great reverence for the mightiest intellectual genius that ever lived and gave to the world the efforts of his wonderful fancy, which are destined to instruct and amuse the children of men as long as the language in which they are written lasts.

More sanguine responses to Delia Bacon's arguments have inspired a shelfful of cryptology books and a series of archaeological expeditions, some of them clandestine. Acting on cryptic messages she deciphered from Bacon's letters, Delia Bacon herself managed to smuggle a small shovel into Holy Trinity Church, Stratford-upon-Avon, with intent to pry up Shakespeare's gravestone and bring to light the will and other documents that Bacon's letters told her she would find underneath. At the moment of taking shovel in hand, she thought the better of it. Other Baconians have been less restrained. Early in the 20th century Dr. Orville Ward Owen of Detroit masterminded, mostly with other people's money, a number of digs in the region of Chepstow on the Wye River. From ciphers he and his assistants had decoded in Shakespeare's works, Owen was convinced he would find a set of iron boxes containing Bacon manuscripts that would settle the authorship question once and for all. In the most recent incident, in September 1991, three members of the Ministry of the Children, a New Age religious group based in Santa Fe, New Mexico, journeyed to Williamsburg, Virginia, to test the theory that a descendant of Francis Bacon had come to Virginia in the late 17th century, bringing with him copper cylinders containing precious unpublished works by his famous ancestor, which he buried under the foundations of Bruton Parish Church. Marie Bauer Hall, who first pieced together the story from ciphers and anagrams and carried out her own unsuccessful excavations at Williamsburg in 1938, inspired the New Age archaeologists with her claim that the buried manuscripts not only would prove Bacon's claim to Shakespeare's plays but would provide a plan for universal peace, for "a true and enlightened world and family Christianity different from anything that we know," in the words of one of the Santa Fe pilgrims. Bacon arranged for his works to be transferred to Virginia, Hall had explained, because he believed that only in the new world could the new order he envisioned be established, and he specified that the works had to be revealed before the end of the 20th century. *Novum Organum* meets New Age. After a legal confrontation with the Ministry of the Children, the vestry of Bruton Parish Church sponsored their own excavation of the original building's foundations. No cylinders or manuscripts were found.

Veering toward Oxford

With the man from Stratford out of the way, claimants other than Francis Bacon—more than fifty of them—have been pushed forward by modern-day advocates. The rival who has proved the most assertive is not Sir Walter Raleigh, not Christopher Marlowe, not Queen Elizabeth, but Edward de Vere, seventeenth Earl of Oxford (1550–1604). The book that can be credited with turning theatrical chitchat into an organized religion is *"Shakespeare" Identified* (London: C. Palmer, 1920) by J. Thomas Looney (1870–1944). (That's pronounced "loan-y," by the way, not "luny.") The Earl of Oxford, famous in literary history only for having written a handful of love poems and for having called Sir Philip Sidney a "puppy" in a dispute on the tennis court, nonetheless fit to a V the authorial profile that Looney deduced from the works attributed to "Shakespeare." Only a man of superior education, an aristocrat with Lancastrian sympathies, who was indifferent to money matters, who knew Italy first hand, who pursued the noble sport of falconry, etc., etc., could have written these plays and poems. A believer in the positivism of Auguste Comte (1798–1857), Looney claimed to have arrived at his list of traits by strictly objective observation. To Looney's deductive logic George Frisbee added crypto-logic in *Edward De Vere: A Great Elizabethan* (London: C. Palmer, 1931), a book that set out to do for Oxford what Dr. Owen and others had done for Bacon. Clues to Oxford's authorship, Frisbee argued, are encoded in the letters D-E-V-E-R-E, not only in the plays attributed to Shakespeare but in works by Marlowe, Raleigh, Spenser, and James I.

The "Oxford Movement" continues as vigorously today as it ever did, long after most Baconians have retreated to the sidelines. Looney's *"Shakespeare" Identified* has gone through three editions (1920, 1949, 1975), the most recent accompanied by a second volume that anthologizes a variety of writers' arguments in favor of Edward de Vere. Furthermore, a personal champion has stepped forward in Charles Francis Topham de Vere Beauclerk, the current Earl of Burford and a collateral descendant of the seventeenth Earl of Oxford. Under Burford's patronage, the Shakespeare Oxford Society publishes a regular *Newsletter*,

Sir Max Beerbohm, "William Shakespeare, His Method of Work," colored lithograph from *The Poets' Corner* (London: W. Heinemann, 1904). Gossip about Oxford as the true author of Shakespeare's plays was current enough in turn-of-the-century theatrical circles for Max Beerbohm (1872–1956) to make satiric capital out of it in his sketch of Oxford slipping Shakespeare a copy of *Hamlet*.

WILLIAM SHAKESPEARE, HIS ᴏMETHOD OF WORK.

sponsors public lectures, and lobbies meetings of the Shakespeare Association of America. In fall 1992 it organized a live, nationwide video-conference on the issue, chaired by William F. Buckley, Jr.

Among the pieces of evidence cited by Oxfordians in support of their cause, the most recent is a Folger copy of the Geneva Bible (1596) in a binding that bears the Earl of Oxford's arms and that is filled with underlinings and annotations in a 16th-century hand. Roger Stritmatter has argued in *The Shakespeare Oxford Society Newsletter*, 29.2A (spring 1993), and in statements to the press that many of the underlined passages are echoed in the plays attributed to Shakespeare. Take, for example, Falstaff's complaint in *The Merry Wives of Windsor* that Master Ford beat him up in the guise of a woman: "I will tell you, he beat me grievously in the shape of a woman—for in the shape of man, Master Brooke, I fear not Goliath with a weaver's beam, because I know also life is a shuttle" (5.1.18–22). This obscure reference to an equally obscure passage in II Samuel 21:19–20 turns out to be underlined (albeit faintly) in the Earl of Oxford's Bible:

19 And there was yet *another* battel in Gob with the Philistins, where E'hanah the sonne of Iarre-oregim, a Bethlehemite slewe Goliath the Gittite: <u>the staffe of whose speare *was* like a weavers beame</u>.

20 Afterwarde was also a battel in Gath, <u>where was a man of *great* stature, and had on everie hand six fingers, and on everie foote six toes</u>, foure and twentie in nomber: who was also the sonne of Haraphah.

(The Bible and Holy Scriptures
[Geneva: J. Crispin, 1596], pp. 153–154)

The Merry Wives makes no mention of Falstaff's having six fingers and toes, but he certainly figures there as "a man of great stature." The annotator's sustained interest in biblical passages having to do with corrupt rulership and with usury might indeed be understandable for a writer of history plays and *The Merchant of Venice*. Against such evidence one has to note that, among the twenty-eight instances in which the annotator has written something in the outer margins, the binder's knife has cut away part of the inscription eighteen times. That would suggest that the annotations were made sometime before the Bible was bound for the Earl of Oxford.

If cryptological proofs are likely to seem convincing only to other cipher-punks, if philological arguments can be disputed by other philologists, if allegories of historical events need a masterkey that not every historian will accept, then clearly what is needed to settle the matter is a panel of impartial judges. Bacon's case was heard by a "Tribunal of Literary Criticism" set up in the pages of the Boston monthly *Arena* in 1892. After more than a year of contributions *pro* and *con* Bacon (but mostly *con*), a panel of judges that included the actor Sir Henry Irving decided overwhelmingly for Shakespeare. Oxford's case has been heard more recently. Three justices of the Supreme Court of the United States—Harry A. Blackmun, William Brennan, and John Paul Stevens—presided in 1987 over a moot-court debate at American University that was underwritten by David Lloyd Kreeger, a noted benefactor of theater in Washington, D.C., and a convinced Oxfordian. A full transcription of the proceedings, held before an audience numbering at least a thousand, was published in the *American University Law Review* 37.3 (1988). Weighing the evidence presented by two American University law professors, all three justices decided for Shakespeare, although Justice Stevens expressed personal uncertainties based largely on his observation "that there are just too many places in which nobility is stressed as a standard" (825). He went on to note, however, that "the Oxford

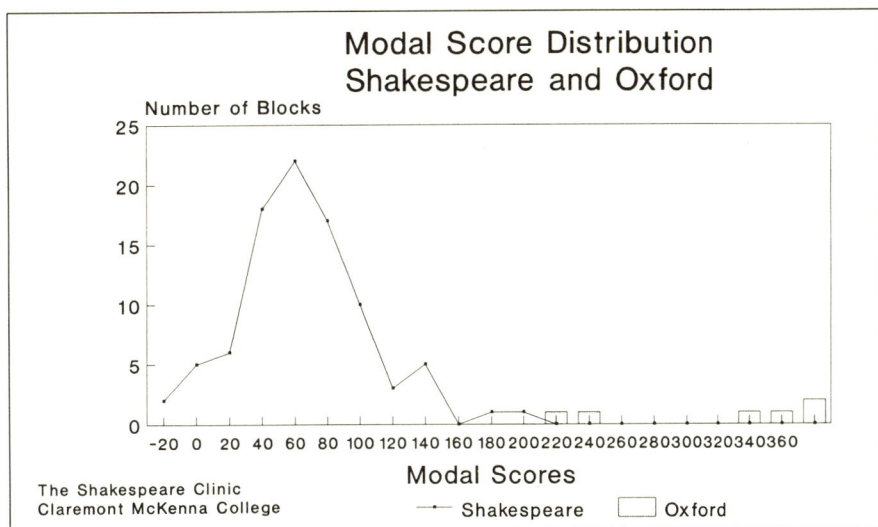

Modal Score Distribution
Shakespeare and Oxford

Number of Blocks

Modal Scores

The Shakespeare Clinic
Claremont McKenna College

—•— Shakespeare   ☐ Oxford

case suffers from not having a single, coherent theory of the case. When pressed, the Oxfordians respond with too many alternatives that might be true or might not be true" (826). When a reprise of the trial was staged at the Middle Temple in London a year later, the three presiding Law Lords likewise found for Shakespeare.

Opinions handed down by the Shakespeare courts in Washington and London have been confirmed in diagnoses offered by the Shakespeare Clinic at Claremont McKenna College in California. In a series of computer-assisted analyses, Ward Elliott and Robert Valenza have isolated word patterns in texts by twenty-seven of the fifty-eight claimants to the title of "Shakespeare." Rather than simply counting repetitions of keywords favored by these authors, Elliott and Valenza have identified the ways in which each of the writers deviates from his or her most frequent uses of those keywords. The resulting "modes" become a way of measuring internal consistency among all texts by a single writer as well as differences from texts by other writers. (To ensure equitable comparison among texts of varying lengths, the texts are first divided up into "blocks" of a standard number of words.)
As Elliott and Valenza put it,

> None of our tests can show that anybody wrote anything. But they can show that someone did *not* write something. They are like Cinderella's slipper. A misfit is strong evidence that you are not Cinderella, but a fit does not necessarily prove that you are Cinderella.[8]

8. Ward Elliott and Robert Valenza, "Who Was Shakespeare?", *Chance: New Directions for Statistics and Computing* 4.3 (1991): 11, emphasis added.

Measured by modes, the plays and poems ascribed to Shakespeare show not only remarkable internal consistency among themselves but remarkable differences from the works of all twenty-seven other writers—including the Earl of Oxford.

Deconstructors

The plays printed in *Mr. William Shakespeares Comedies, Histories, & Tragedies* (1623) have maintained their canonical status down to the present moment, but on the whole 20th-century criticism has not been kind to Mr. William Shakespeare himself. The first rebuff, mild as it may have been, came from the "New Criticism" of the 1940s and 50s. With its insistent focus on close scrutiny of texts at the expense of history and biography, New Criticism needed Shakespeare only as the off-stage author of well wrought texts that set up tensions between opposites. From there Shakespeare's authorial career has been in continuous decline. The political assumptions that propped up his prestige are exposed in Terry Eagleton's *Literary Theory: An Introduction* (Minneapolis: University of Minnesota Press, 1976). In *The Four Fundamental Concepts of Psycho-analysis* (English edition, New York: Norton, 1978) Jacques Lacan has demonstrated how "I" is always a function of language and culture, hence calling into question just how much we in the postmodern present have in common with the early modern characters who speak in Shakespeare's scripts or the "I" who speaks in the sonnets. Catherine Belsey's *Critical Practice* (New York: Methuen, 1980) tells would-be deconstructors how to do the job. The ultimate insult was delivered as long ago as 1968 by Roland Barthes, who in an essay in *Image-Music-Text* (English edition, New York: Hill & Wang, 1977) confidently announced "The Death of the Author": "We now know that a text is not a line of words releasing a single 'theological' meaning (the 'message' of an Author-God) but a multi-dimensional space in which a variety of writings, none of them original, blend and clash" (p. 146). To fill the existential void left by the author, Barthes instates the reader. Promoted to this new position of power, the reader can refuse the designs that a text makes upon her. Instead of wholeness and clarity, she can look out for contradictions, for the clash of meanings that Barthes talks about. In effect, the reader can "deconstruct" the text. Long before Jacques Derrida appeared on the academic scene, however, Shakespeare was already being deconstructed both literally and figuratively. An early-17th century manuscript at Alnwick Castle, Northumberland, not only intersperses plays by Shakespeare with

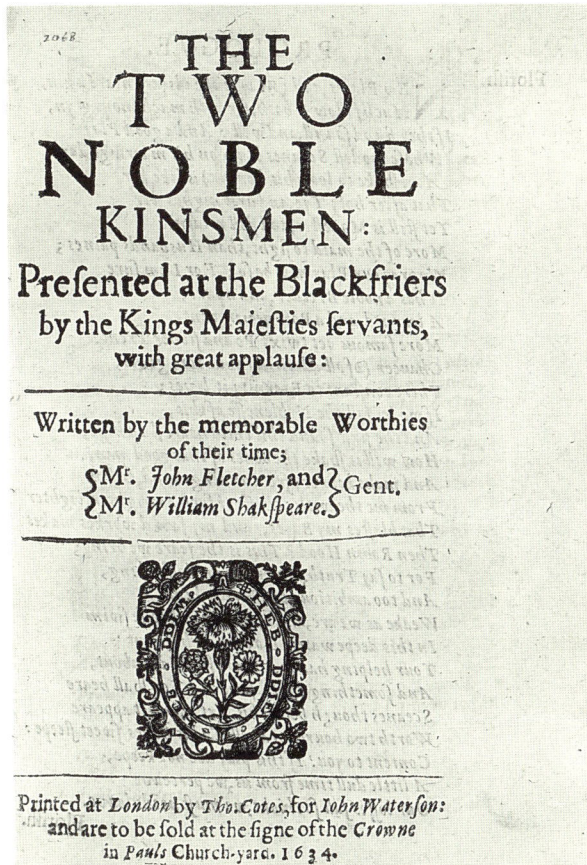

THE
TWO
NOBLE
KINSMEN:
Prefented at the Blackfriers
by the Kings Maiefties fervants,
with great applaufe:

Written by the memorable Worthies
of their time;
{ Mr. *John Fletcher*, and } Gent.
{ Mr. *William Shakſpeare*. }

Printed at *London* by *Tho.Cotes*, for *Iohn Waterſon*:
and are to be fold at the figne of the *Crowne*
in *Pauls* Church-yard. 1 6 3 4.

John Fletcher and William Shakespeare, *The Two Noble Kinsmen* (London: Thomas Cotes for John Waterson, 1634), title page. The brackets on each side of the two authors' names point up a crisis in traditional aesthetic criticism.

texts by (of all people) Francis Bacon, but an early reader has heightened the effect of authorial erasure by breaking up Shakespeare's name into doodles.

Can a masterpiece have two authors? Can a "doubtful" work crash the canon? The brackets on Waterson's title page call into question Shakespeare's authority, individuality, and credibility—in a word, his *integrity*. Although it must have been acted as early as 1613 or 1614, *The Two Noble Kinsmen* was not printed until 1634. The play had not appeared in the First Folio of Shakespeare's plays in 1623 (possibly because of copyright problems); neither was it included in *Comedies and Tragedies Written by Francis Beaumont and John Fletcher, Gentlemen* in 1647 (perhaps because it was already in print). In relation both to Shakespeare's published works and to Fletcher's, then, the play presents an awkward anomaly. In Michael Bristol's words, "*The Two Noble Kinsmen* approaches the canon from without, like an uninvited guest, a stranger with familiar features."[9] Despite stylistic evidence that substantiates the claims of Waterson's title page, *The Two Noble Kinsmen* was not included in any of the great

9. Michael D. Bristol, "*The Two Noble Kinsmen*: Shakespeare and the Problem of Authority," in Charles H. Frey, ed., *Shakespeare, Fletcher, and The Two Noble Kinsmen* (Columbia: University of Missouri Press, 1989), p. 84.

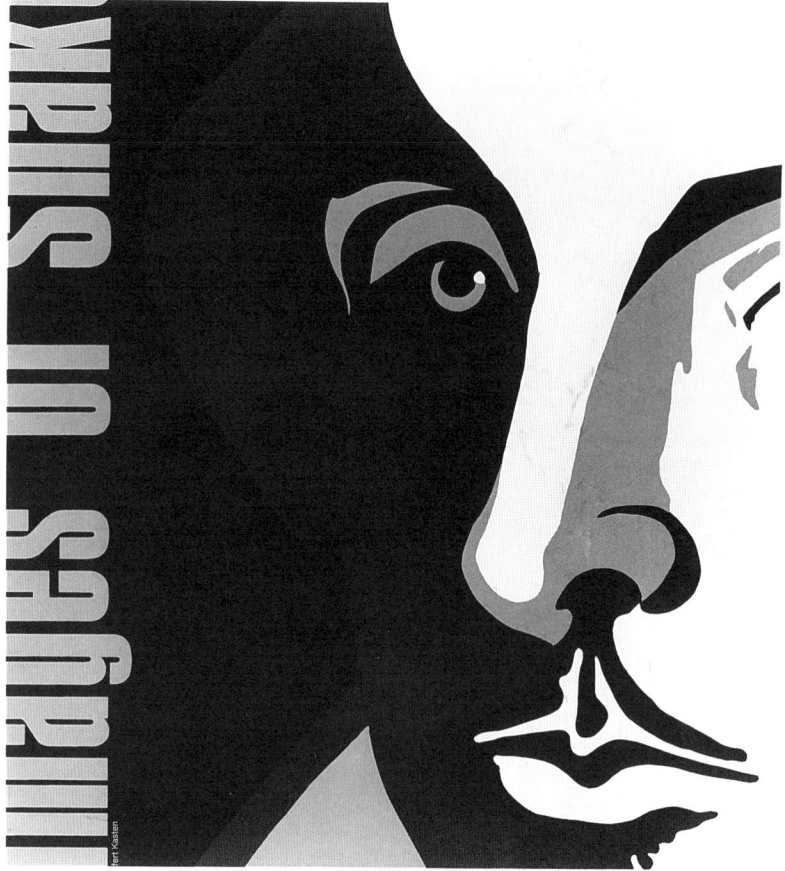

Ulfert Kasten (b. 1959), Poster (detail) for 1986 International Shakespeare Congress, Berlin, courtesy of Prof.-Dr. Kuno Schuhmann, Technische Universität, Berlin. During the course of the 20th century Shakespeare has suffered increasingly from I-trouble.

18th- and 19th-century collected editions of Shakespeare's works. It even has failed to make such widely used 20th-century editions as the Arden and the Pelican.

Whatever the case with *The Two Noble Kinsmen*, accidents of publishing may in other respects have contributed to Shakespeare's posthumous success. In *Reinventing Shakespeare* (New York: Weidenfeld & Nicolson, 1989), Gary Taylor observes how the historical William Shakespeare has disappeared under the meanings heaped upon him by later generations:

> If Shakespeare has a singularity, it is because he has become a black hole. Light, insight, intelligence, matter— all pour ceaselessly into him, as critics are drawn into the densening vortex of his reputation; they add their own weight to his increasing mass. The light from other stars—other poets, other dramatists—is wrenched and bent as it passes by him on its way to us. (p. 410)

George L. Gray, *Shakespeare Boiled Down* (Chicago: New Home Sewing Machine Co., [n.d.]). For busy homemakers the New Home Sewing Machine Company provided this early 20th-century equivalent of later deconstructions like *Cliff's Notes* and Shakespeare on video. The introduction points out that the author "has not tried to be eloquent, copy Shakespeare's unequaled style of writing, or quote any of his quaint expressions." *Shakespeare Boiled Down* yields a shelf of halfpint short stories, followed by a catalog of New Home's line of sewing machines. In the table of contents "Romeo and Juliet" is succeeded by "Strong Points in Favor of the New Home," a plausible plotline if Nahum Tate had got hold of the play (see **...and Nature Redressed**).

SHAKESPERE

BOILED DOWN.

COPYRIGHT 1890 BY GEO. L. GRAY.

...WRITTEN AND PUBLISHED EXPRESSLY FOR THE...

NEW HOME SEWING MACHINE CO.

CHICAGO, ILL.

Among those eclipsed stars the brightest may be Thomas Middleton, whose reputation Taylor is championing in a new collected edition of his plays. One reason Middleton's name is never carved next to Shakespeare's on the friezes of Carnegie libraries may be the simple fact that he, unlike Shakespeare, was not lucky enough to have had his works collected in folio. The closest he ever came before the 19th century is *Two New Plays, viz. More Dissemblers Besides Women, Women Beware Women* (London: for Humphrey Moseley, 1657), published thirty years after his death. By then, the Swan of Avon was already a fixture in cultural history.

Famous Last Words

The last word is a swan's,

as transcribed by Orlando Gibbons (1583–1625) in one of the most famous among his *First Set of Madrigals and Motets* (London: Thomas Snodham, 1612):

> The silver swan, who living had no note
> When death approached, unlocked her silent throat,
> Leaning her breast against the reedy shore,
> Thus sang her first and last, and sung no more:
> Farewell all joys. O Death, come close mine eyes.
> *More geese than swans now live, more fools than wise.*

Silvester Harding (1745–1809), "The Spirit of Shakspere Appearing to his Detractors" (1796), engraving. Harding had his eye on particular detractors and particular incidents, else he would have needed the space of a Great Hall for his gallery of rogues. The "detractors" here are Samuel and William Henry Ireland (see **Forgery: Flattery or Fraud?**). Harding has imitated their scam by providing a spurious caption: "Design'd & engraved by W. Hogarth & found by somebody in an old Chest."

ITEMS INCLUDED IN THE EXHIBITION

(Items displayed on the wall are listed under the adjacent case.)

Case 1: Eating Crow

Robert Greene (attributed), *Greens Groats-worth of Wit* (London: Thomas Creede, 1596), STC 12246.

William Shakespeare, *The True Tragedie of Richarde Duke of Yorke* (London: W. W. for T. Millington, 1600), STC 21006a Copy 1.

Horace, *Poemata* (London: John Norton, 1608), STC 13791.2.

Laurens Van Haecht Goidtsenhoven (text) and Jacob de Zetter (illustrations), *Microcosmos* (Frankfurt: Lucas Jennis, 1618), PN 6349 M4 1618 Cage.

Richard Tarlton (attributed), "A Prettie Newe Ballad, Intytuled: The Crowe Sits Upon the Wall" (London: for Henry Kyrkham, 1592), STC 23683 (reproduced from British Library, Huth Collection, fol. 31).

Henry Chettle, *Kind-Harts Dreame* (London: for William Wright, 1593?), STC 5123.

Case 2: "Sweet Swan of Avon"—with a Grain of Salt

William Shakespeare, *Mr. William Shakespeares Comedies, Histories, & Tragedies. Published according to the True Originall Copies* (London: Isaac Jaggard and Edward Blount, 1623), STC 22273.

Unknown mid-18th century artist, Portrait of Ben Jonson, possibly after Peter Oliver, oil on canvas, Pressly 191. Gift of the Trustees of the Cleveland Museum of Art in Memory of Mr. and Mrs. James Parmalee, 1940.

Ben Jonson, *The Workes of Benjamin Jonson* (London: for R. Meighen, 1640), STC 14754 Copy 2.

William Drummond, *Poems* (Edinburgh: Andro Hart, 1616), STC 7255 Copy 2, with tipped-in portrait.

Ben Jonson, *The Workes of Benjamin Jonson* (London: T. Harper, 1641), STC 14754a Copy 1.

Unknown late 19th-century artist, Shakespeare's coat-of-arms, oil on canvas, Pressly 202.

Case 3: Railers and Scourgers

John Davies, *The Scourge of Folly* (London: E. A. for Richard Redmer, 1611), STC 6341 Copy 1.

Ratseis Ghost. Or the Second Part of His Madde Prankes and Robberies (London: V. S., 1605), STC 20753a, title page reproduced from the unique copy in the John Rylands Library, Manchester.

John Webster, *The White Devil* (London: N. O. for Thomas Archer, 1612), STC 25178.

Robert Anton, *The Philosopher's Satyrs* (London: T. C. and B. A. for Roger Jackson, 1616), STC 686.

Wits Recreations (London: for Humphrey Blunden, 1640), STC 25870 Copy 2.

Case 4: Playing the Sodomite—or Worse

Print after Pieter Breughel the Elder, *The Village Fair of Hoboken* (1559). Lent by the National Gallery of Art, Rosenwald Collection.

Philip Stubbs, *The Anatomie of Abuses* (London: Richard Jones, 1583), STC 23377.

William Prynne, *Histrio-Mastix. The Players Scourge, or, Actors Tragedie* (London: E. A. and W. I. for Michael Sparke, 1633), STC 20464a Copy 2.

Wenceslaus Hollar, Portrait of William Prynne, engraving (undated), acc. 234100

Accomack County, Virginia, Order Book for 1663–1666, fol. 102, reproduced from the original in the Virginia State Library, Richmond.

Abraham de Bruyn, *Omnium Pene Europae, Asiae, Aphricae . . . Gentium Habitus* (Antwerp: Michiel Colÿn, 1581), GT 513 B81581 Cage.

Case 5: Nature Dressed . . .

George Romney, *The Infant Shakespeare, Attended by Nature and the Passions*, engraved by Benjamin Smith, published by John and Josiah Boydell, colored engraving (1799), Art Flat b1 Copy 1.

John Milton, *Poems* (London: R. Raworth for H. Moseley, 1645), M 2160 Copy 1.

Francis Beaumont and John Fletcher, *Comedies and Tragedies* (London: for Humphrey Robinson and Humphrey Moseley, 1647), B 1581.

William Cartwright, *Comedies, Tragi-comedies, with Other Poems* (London: Humphrey Moseley, 1651), C 709 Copy 1.

Charles Dibdin, "Sweet Willy O," from *Jubilee, or Shakespear's Garland* (London: John Johnston, 1769), Black Music Box VIII, Charles Dibdin File.

Samuel Ireland, "Stratford Church &c," from *Picturesque Views on the Upper or Warwickshire Avon* (1795), Art File S898c1 No. 14.

William Faithorne, Portrait of William D'Avenant, after John Greenhill, engraving (1672), Art File D246.3 No. 1.

John Thomas Blight, The Crown Inn, Oxford, pencil and watercolor on paper, Art Vol. d78 No. 7b.

Case 6: . . . and Nature Redressed

John Dryden, *Troilus and Cressida, or Truth Found too Late* (London: for Jacob Tonson and Abel Swall, 1679), D 2388 Copy 1.

Jonathan Richardson, Portrait of John Dryden, pencil on vellum (c. 1730), Pressly 196.

William Shakespeare, *Mr. William Shakespeares Comedies, Histories, & Tragedies. The Second Impression* (London: Thomas Cotes, 1632), Folio 2 Fragment B2.

John Dryden and William D'Avenant, *The Tempest, or The Enchanted Island* (London: J. M. for Henry Herringman, 1670), S 2944 Copy 4.

Nahum Tate, *The History of King Lear* (London: E. Flesher, 1681), S 2918 Copy 2.

Francis Hayman, design for engraving of *King Lear*, Act 3, scene 6, ink on paper, tipped into *The Works of Mr. William Shakespear*, ed. Sir Thomas Hanmer (Oxford: Oxford University Press, 1744), PR 2752 1744 Copy 2 Vol. 3 Sh. Col.

George Granville, *The Jew of Venice* (London: for Bernard Lintot and B. Motte, 1732), PR 3539 L4 J4 1732 Cage.

Case 7: Breaking the Quill

William Shakespeare, *The Most Excellent and Lamentable Tragedie, of Romeo and Juliet* (London: for John Smethwicke, [1622]), STC 22325a.

William Shakespeare, *Supplement to the Edition of Shakespeare's Plays Published in 1778*, ed. Edmond Malone (London: C. Bathurst, 1780), PR 2752 1778 Suppl. 1 Copy 5.

William Shakespeare, *Sonnets*, intro. W. H. Auden (New York: New American Library, 1964).

Henrietta Maria Bowdler, ed., *The Family Shakespeare* (London: for J. Hatchard, 1807), PR 2752 1807g Copy 2 Vol. 1 Sh. Col.

Henrietta Maria Bowdler, letter to a "Miss Gorman" in Dublin (17 July 1818), MS Add 864.

Thomas Bowdler, letter to Sir William Hamilton (1 June 1781), MS Y.c.248 (1).

Fannie Safier, gen. ed., *Adventures in Reading: Heritage Edition* (Orlando: Harcourt Brace Jovanovich, 1980). Copy lent by Elizabeth Gaudin.

G. B. Trudeau, Doonesbury cartoon on censorship of *Romeo and Juliet* (31 March 1985). Copy lent by G. B. Trudeau.

Case 8: Forgery: Flattery or Fraud?

John Nixon, "The Oaken Chest or The Gold Mines of Ireland, a Farce," colored engraving (1797) Art File S527.6 no. 2 Copy 1.

Supposed fan letter from Queen Elizabeth to William Shakespeare, MS W.b.496, fol. 105.

The First Part of the True & Honorable History, of the Life of Sir John Old-castle . . . (London: for T.P., 1600 [for 1619]), STC 18796 Copy 2.

Cupid's Cabinet Unlock't (n.p., nd. [before 1700]),
C 7597a.

Samuel Ireland, *Miscellaneous Papers and Legal
Instruments under the Hand and Seal of William
Shakspeare . . . from the Original MSS. in the Possession of
Samuel Ireland, of Norfolk Street* (London: published by
subscription, 1796), PR 2950 A22a Cage Copy 2, with
tipped-in portrait of Samuel Ireland, engraved by
himself, after Hugh Douglas Hamilton.

Supposed letter from William Shakespeare to Anne
Hathaway enclosing a lock of his hair, MS W.b.496,
fol. 93.

Unknown 19th-century artist, Portrait of John Payne
Collier, engraved image reproduced in photogravure,
Art File C699.5.

Commonplace book, c. 1630–1640, with forgeries by
John Payne Collier, MS V.a.339.

Case 9: Shakespeare Sacrificed

Henry Fuseli, *A Midsummer Night's Dream*,
Act 4, Scene 1, engraved by Peter Simon, Plate 20 in *A
Collection of Prints from Pictures Painted for the Purpose of
Illustrating the Dramatic Works of Shakespeare by the
Artists of Great Britain* (London: John and Josiah
Boydell, 1803), Art Flat b1 Copy 1.

James Gillray, "Shakespeare-Sacrificed; or The
Offering to Avarice," acquatint (1789), Art File S527.6
no. 3a Copy 1.

James Gillray, "The Monster Broke Loose, or a Peep
into the Shakespeare-Gallery," acquatint (1791),
Art Flat a5 No. 3.

Chelsea Gold Anchor porcelain, Standing statue of
Shakespeare (1758–69), Art Curio 234198.

William Shakespeare, *Plays*, ed. Samuel Johnson
(London: J. and R. Tonson, 1765), PR 2752 1765a Copy 3
Sh. Col. Vols. 1-8.

Thomas Rowlandson, *Macbeth* in Performance, pen
and ink and watercolor on paper, Art Box R883 No. 1.

Georg Emanuel Opiz, Backstage scene from *Hamlet*, watercolor on paper, Art Box O61 No. 2.

Unknown 18th-century artist, Shakespeare Jubilee Parade (1769), watercolor on paper, Art Vol. D94 No. 83a.

Ceramic cup (c. 1750) showing "Shakespeare's mulberry tree," Art Curio.

Thomas Sharp, rolling pin made from wood saved from Shakespeare's mulberry tree, Wood No. 1.

"Shakespeere's Mulberry Tree" (c. 1769), Art Vol. d94, fol. 89.

Unknown 18th-century artist, Portrait miniature of the Reverend Francis Gastrell. Lent by the Shakespeare Birthplace Trust, Stratford-upon-Avon.

Case 10: Ungenial Geniuses

P. G. Langlois, after Maurice Quentin de La Tour, Portrait of François Marie Arouet de Voltaire, engraving, Art File V935 No. 1.

François Marie Arouet de Voltaire, *Letters Concerning the English Nation* (London: C. Davis and A. Lyon, 1733), PQ 2086 L4 E5 1733 Cage.

Lev Nikolaevich Tolstoi, reproduction of contemporary photograph. Lent by Prof. Zelda Teplitz, Georgetown University.

Lev Nikolaevich Tolstoi, *Tolstoy on Shakespeare*, trans. V. Tchertkoff and I. F. M. (New York and London: Funk and Wagnalls, 1906), PR 2979 R9 T7.

Joseph Clayton Clarke ("Kyd"), "G. B. Shaw 'Cutting' Shakespeare in Hades," watercolor and ink on paper, Art Box C598 No. 4.

George Bernard Shaw, *Dramatic Opinions and Essays* (London: Constable, 1907), PN 2594 S5.

George Bernard Shaw, *The Dark Lady of the Sonnets: An Interlude*, published with inscription "Rough Proof—Unpublished" (London: Constable, 1910), PR 2935 S4.

Mrs. Patrick Campbell as Ophelia in 1897, contemporary photograph, Art File C190 No. 2.

Case 11: "What in Hell Did He Ever Do for Denver?"

Thomas Nast, Study for *The Immortal Light of Genius*, oil on paper laid down on canvas (1895), Pressly 201.

Advertisement for "Thos. Nast in His Artistic Entertainment Drawing in Black and White and Painting in OIL Colors in Presence of the Audience" (probably 1887), Art Flat a25 Pt. 10 Copy 3.

William Heath, "The Rival Richards, or Sheakspear in Danger," colored engraving (1814), Art File K24.4 No. 89.

Mark Twain, *Adventures of Huckleberry Finn* (New York: Charles L. Webster and Co., 1885). Lent by Prof. John Hirsh, Georgetown University.

Esquire magazine, March 1993.

Sir Bernard Partridge, "Uncle Sam" stealing British masterpieces, pencil and ink on paper, Art Box P275 No. 1.

Henry Clay Folger, assorted correspondence with Henry Sotheran & Co., London, 1903, relating to purchase of *Mr. William Shakespeares Comedies, Histories, & Tragedies* (1623), Folio 1 Copy 1.

Tom Phillips, "Shakespeare in America," limited-edition poster for the 1976 International Shakespeare Congress, Washington, D.C., Art P857 No. 2 Copy 1.

Case 12: Egging On Bacon

Joseph Clayton Clarke ("Kyd"), Shakespeare and Bacon, watercolor and ink on paper, Art Box C598 No. 2.

Delia Bacon, reproduction of contemporary photograph.

Delia Bacon, *The Philosophy of the Plays of Shakspere Unfolded* (Boston: Ticknor and Fields, 1857), PR 2944 B2 P7 Copy 2.

Delia Bacon, letter to Nathaniel Hawthorne, MS Y.c.2599 No. 90.

Nathaniel Hawthorne, letter to Delia Bacon, MS Y.c.2599 No. 214.

Scrapbook of Shakespeareana assembled by J. Woods Poinier Jr. of New York City, 1872–1876.

Richmond [Virginia] Times-Dispatch, 15 September 1991, with stories about excavations carried out by the Ministry of the Children at Williamsburg, Virginia.

Case 13: Veering toward Oxford

Sir Max Beerbohm, "William Shakespeare, His Method of Work," colored lithograph from *The Poets' Corner* (London: W. Heinemann, 1904), Art Vol. f3.

J. Thomas Looney, *"Shakespeare" Identified* (London: C. Palmer, 1920), PR 2947 O9 L6 1920.

George Frisbee, *Edward De Vere: A Great Elizabethan* (London: C. Palmer, 1931), PR 2947 O9 F7.

The Bible and Holy Scriptures (Geneva: J. Crispin, 1596), STC 2106.

The Shakespeare Oxford Society Newsletter, vol. 29, no. 2A (spring 1993), together with assorted flyers and brochures.

American University Law Review, vol. 37, no. 3 (1988), PR 2947 O9 I6.

Ward Elliott and Robert Valenza, Graph showing computer-assisted comparison of word frequencies for Shakespeare and Oxford.

Case 14: Deconstructors

Alnwick Castle MS (Northumberland MS) containing works by Shakespeare and Bacon, photographic reproduction of fol. 1 in Francis Bacon, *A Conference of Pleasure*, ed. James Spedding (London: Whittingham and Wilkins, 1870), PR 2206 C4 S8.

Jacques Derrida, *Of Grammatology* (Baltimore: Johns Hopkins University Press, 1976).

Terry Eagleton, *Literary Theory: An Introduction* (Minneapolis: University of Minnesota Press, 1976).

Jacques Lacan, *The Four Fundamental Concepts of Psycho-analysis* (New York: Norton, 1978).

Catherine Belsey, *Critical Practice* (New York: Methuen, 1980).

Roland Barthes, *Image-Music-Text* (New York: Hill & Wang, 1977).

John Fletcher and William Shakespeare, *The Two Noble Kinsmen* (London: Thomas Cotes for John Waterson, 1634), STC 11075 Copy 1.

Thomas Middleton, *Two New Plays, viz. More Dissemblers Besides Women, Women Beware Women* (London: for Humphrey Moseley, 1657), M 1989.

George L. Gray, *Shakespeare Boiled Down* (Chicago: New Home Sewing Machine Co., [n.d.]), Sh. Misc. 776.

Gary Carey, ed., *Cliff's Notes on Shakespeare's Minor Plays* (Lincoln, Nebraska: Cliff's Notes Co., 1991).

Ulfert Kasten, Poster for 1986 International Shakespeare Congress, Berlin. Courtesy of Prof.-Dr. Kuno Schuhmann, Technische Universität, Berlin.

Famous Last Words

Orlando Gibbons, *First Set of Madrigals and Motets* (London: Thomas Snodham, 1612), STC 11826 Copy 1.

Silvester Harding, "The Spirit of Shakspere Appearing to his Detractors," engraving (1796), Art File S527.6 No. 1.

SUGGESTIONS FOR FURTHER READING

There are two book-length surveys of all the things people have done to Shakespeare: S. Schoenbaum, *Shakespeare's Lives*, rev. edition (Oxford: Clarendon Press, 1991), and Gary Taylor, *Reinventing Shakespeare* (New York: Weidenfeld & Nicolson, 1989). Schoenbaum's book has been particularly important to the preparation of "Roasting the Swan of Avon."

Responses to Shakespeare's plays—critical and otherwise—from 1591 to 1700 are collected in *The Shakspere* [sic] *Allusion-Book*, compiled by C. M. Ingleby, L. Toulmin Smith, and F. J. Furnivall and revised by John Munro and E. K. Chambers, 2 vols. (1932; rpt. Freeport, N.Y.: Books for Libraries, 1970). The record is amplified and continued down to 1801 in the six volumes of *Shakespeare: The Critical Heritage*, ed. Brian Vickers (London: Routledge, 1974–1981). Essays on how Shakespeare has been drafted and redrafted for causes and concerns ranging from Restoration stage productions to drip-mats for beer are collected in Jean I. Marsden, ed., *The Appropriation of Shakespeare* (London: Harvester Wheatsheaf, 1991). On the 18th-century reinvention of Shakespeare as a paragon of middle-class values (largely through the ways his works were edited and printed) see Colin Franklin, *Shakespeare Domesticated* (Aldershot: Scolar Press, 1991), and Margreta de Grazia, *Shakespeare Verbatim* (Oxford: Clarendon Press, 1991). The role of "improved" versions of Shakespeare's plays in this process of cultural transformation is studied by Michael Dobson in *The Making of the National Poet* (Oxford: Clarendon Press, 1992). On the Stratford festivities of 1769 a reader has a choice between *Garrick's Jubilee* by Martha Winburn England (Columbus: Ohio State University Press, 1964) and *Garrick's Folly* by Johanne M. Stockholm (New York: Barnes & Noble, 1964). The stratagems that 18th- and 19th-century commentators used to avoid the embarrassing subject of homoeroticism in Shakespeare's sonnets are surveyed by Peter Stallybrass in "Editing as Cultural Formation: The Sexing of Shakespeare's Sonnets," *Modern Language Quarterly* 54.1 (1993): 91-103. Contexts for these shifts in critical perspective, from the late 18th century to the present, are set in place by Hugh Grady, *The Modernist Shakespeare* (Oxford: Clarendon Press, 1991). American capitalizations on Shakespeare are the subject of Michael D. Bristol's *Shakespeare's America, America's Shakespeare* (London: Routledge, 1990).

Oil paintings included here are more fully described by William L. Pressly, *A Catalogue of Paintings in the Folger Shakespeare Library* (New Haven: Yale University Press, 1993). Winifred H. Friedman's *Boydell's Shakespeare Gallery* (New York: Garland, 1976) provides a thorough account of Boydell's print-publishing venture—and of the satiric images that the venture inspired.

Reasons why contemporary critics are theoretically hostile to authors are lucidly explained by Catherine Belsey in *Critical Practice* (New York: Methuen, 1980) and Terry Eagleton in *Literary Theory: An Introduction* (Minneapolis: University of Minnesota Press, 1976).